"My two favorite "happiness" people have written a book about one of the most important topics in organizations: happiness at work. Maartje and Fennande bring science and practice together so that the content is well-founded and practically applicable. They always give me different insights, perspectives, and a hundred new ideas when I talk to them. Plus, a lot of new energy to build a positive work culture. Very inspiring."

~ MONIKA HILM, AUTHOR, PUT YOUR PEOPLE FIRST

"Happiness. We want it, we need it, but what is it? The Ancient Greeks saw it as harmony and balance; their word for it, 'Eudaimonia,' was about seeking fulfillment, the joy that you feel as you strive to reach your potential.

We can't reach that potential alone. We need support from our friends, family, whānau, and the organizations we work for. We need organizations that create an environment that encourages and supports us to achieve our true potential; a place where people are engaged; employees thrive and fulfill the needs of, and delight, their customers. Great outcomes achieved with highly engaged teams is what being agile is all about; a happy place.

Happiness is important but little focussed upon, and Maartje and Fennande's book fills a much-needed gap on the bookshelf. Through their four pillars of Purpose, People, Progress, and Positivity, they (Passionately and Practically!) guide you. Their thought-provoking ideas, supporting research, and small incremental steps will help nudge your work environment to be a place where people can fulfill their true potential.

So sit back, read this book and learn from Maartje and Fennande on how to bring happiness to your workplace. It is a joy to read."

~ANT BOOBIER, AGILE COACH, NOMAD8

"You know what I think about work? I think it's here to stay. Yes, all the changes, developments, upheavals, and shifts we see in the world are going to affect our workplaces – that's forsure. But work will always exist and will always be an important part of our lives.

In the future, we may not work from 9 to 5 or work out of an office... but we will still work. It is a basic expression of who we are as humans to want to do something important, meaningful, and valuable. Not to mention the fact that many of the things we need to live and thrive are only available because someone worked to make them. Everything from the food on your table to the haircut on your head to the latest Marvel movie is the result of work.

So work isn't going anywhere. It is and will stay a fundamental fact of life. And given that, I think it is essential that we make work a good experience. It's incredibly unfair (not to mention incredibly dumb) to accept a state of society where everyone is required to work in order to make a living but where working has an overall negative effect on people. And make no mistake about it, that is the current state of affairs when it comes to work.

Someone should really do something about that.
And this book is a crucial tool for doing it.

I have known Fennande and Maartje for coming up on a decade now, and their dedication to making work better and creating happy offices has been a joy to behold. They're also a couple of really smart people, so the knowledge and tools that they've distilled in this book are absolutely essential.
Read it. And then go create happy offices!"

**~ALEXANDER KJERULF, WOOHOO INC,
AUTHOR, HAPPY HOUR IS 9-5 & LEADING WITH HAPPINESS**

"Happiness at work is a popular topic these days. But it is often still a concept that is difficult to grasp fully. In their book, Maartje and Fennande give a structured framework on how to define it and start working on it.

I have often exchanged thoughts with them on the "Purpose" element in their approach, based on my own experience that this is a crucial element in company culture. A captivating book with lots of practical applicability."

~TIM VANHERCK, HEAD OF HUMAN RESOURCES, JOHNSON & JOHNSON SUPPLY CHAIN EMEA

The Happy Office Manifesto

THE FOUR PILLARS OF A POSITIVE WORK CULTURE

MAARTJE WOLFF &
FENNANDE VAN DER MEULEN

The authors and publishers have made all reasonable efforts to contact copyright-holders for permission, and apologies for any omissions or errors in the form of credits given. Names and details of scenarios in this book have been changed to protect the privacy of individuals and organizations. Corrections may be made to future printings.

Copyright © 2022 Maartje Wolf & Fennande van der Meulen,

All rights reserved. No part of this book may be reproduced or transmitted in any form or by any other means, electronic or mechanical, including photocopying, recording or by any other information storage and retrieval system, without permission of the copyright owner, except for the use of brief quotations in a book review

To request permission, contact the publisher at books@businessagility.institute

ISBN: 978-1-957600-20-8 (Paperback)
ISBN: 978-1-957600-21-5 (Digital Book)

First Paperback Edition: September 2020
Original Title:
Het Happy Office Manifest, de vier pijlers van een gelukkige werkcultuur
Copyright © Happy Office, Business Contact

Edited by: Christopher Ruz
Translation Edited by: Sarah Metcalfe
Layout by: Christopher Morales
Photographs by: Marie van der Heijden
Icons by: https://freeicons.io
Weight Icon by Hilmy Abiyyu Asad
Female Head Icon by www.wishforge.games

Published by:
Business Agility Institute
76 Woodhill, Irvine, CA 92620
Phone: 540-449-2008
businessagility.institute

THANK YOU!

Being grateful is one of the most powerful exercises related to positive psychology. During the creation of his book, we had much to be thankful for. Without a number of people this book would never have become what it is now.

Thank you, Pepijn, for putting us on the track to happiness at work and positive work culture in 2016, and for daring to enter into the adventure with us. Without you there would not have been a 'Happy Office', nor this book!

Thank you, Anne-Marie, for your decisiveness. We had an appointment a few hours after we asked you how to approach a publisher.

Thank you, Harry, for reading with us all those times, for your critical view on content and formulation, your clear opinion on choice of words and the use of professional jargon. And great that ultimately you could accept the use of the word 'purpose'.

Thank you, Janine, for believing in us and your support throughout the entire process: from coming up with our plan up to writing the final version of the manuscript. Thank you also for your upbeat words when we were down and for your rigorous crossing out when the book threatened to become too long. It was special to see how we thought alike in terms of structure, contents, and design. Our collaboration was so smooth and natural.

Thank you, Marloes, for your inspiration concerning the subject mindset. All our conversations, your research, and your comments truly improved the chapter, 'Develop your growth mindset'. Thank you, Franca, for reading with us, for your questions, comments, and immediate feedback. It really helped us a lot at the last moment.

Dearest Hans, Betty, and Monika, thank you for your interest, pride, and moral support. The phone calls and uplifting words have motivated us to persevere.

Also, thanks to Alexander, Joanne, Rich, Dan, Steve, Carole, Sophie, Ammarai, Onno, Arie Pieter, Meike, Hester, Woohoo Partners, Ant, Tim, Evan, Christopher M, Christopher R and Nyssa for your reviews, inspiration, input, contributions, beautiful examples and language corrections and other ways in making this book happen.

And especially thank you, Arie, Joost, and Isa, Ralph and Boaz. We could not have done it without your patience, love and support.

TABLE OF CONTENTS

Chapter 1 - Our Firm Conviction — **19**
The relevance of happiness at work
and a positive work culture — 23

Chapter 2
The Truths and Myths of Happiness at Work — **33**
What is happiness at work? — 34
What is the role of emotions? — 36
The Difference Between Happiness at Work
and Job Satisfaction — 39
What causes unhappiness at work? — 44
Myths About Happiness at Work: What is True? — 45

Chapter 3
The Pillars of Happiness at Work: 4 p's — **49**
Four factors that make us happy — 51
Pillar 1: Purpose — 52
Pillar 2: People — 58
Pillar 3: Progress — 60
Pillar 4: Positivity — 64
The biological side of the four pillars — 70

Chapter 4
A Positive Work Culture is Something
That You Create Together — **73**
Positive work culture — 74
Shared responsibility — 76

Chapter 5
Ownership of Your Happiness at Work — **79**
Self-knowledge and the quadrants of ownership — 79
The effect of the good example — 85

Chapter 6 - Develop Your Growth Mindset   87
What is mindset?   87
Misunderstandings and pitfalls   91
How do you develop a growth mindset?   92

Chapter 7
How You Can Change Your Behavior Permanently   101
Designing behavior makes change easy   101
Motivation   102
Ability   105
Environment   107
Making up for a shortage   109
Effectively designing a change in behavior   109

Chapter 8
Behavior and Happiness at Work:
Focus on the Pillars   111
Improving on – Purpose   113
Improving on people - connection   117
Improvement on progress – satisfaction   120
Improvement on positivity – fun   126
Just try it   130

Chapter 9
The Manager and a Positive Team Culture   131
The mindset of a manager   132
What makes a good leader?   136
How will you get to work with your team?   140
The next step   143

Chapter 10
The Manager or Leader and the
Four Pillars of Happiness at Work   145
Contributing to purpose – meaning   145
Contributing to people – connection   148
Contributing to progress – results   154
Contributing to positivity – fun   161
From team level to organizational level   166

Chapter 11
Building a Positive Organizational Culture   **167**
Zooming in on the term 'organizational culture'   168
Developing an organization culture   171
Step 1. Develop a common language   173
Step 2. Map out the organization   176
The foundation has been laid   180

Chapter 12 - The Culture Change Wheel   183
Step 3. Formulating purpose, core values
and desired behavior   183
Step 4. Getting to work with the Cultural Change Wheel   191

Final Remarks - Getting to Work with the
Right Knowledge and Tools   207

Twelve of Our Favorite Ideas   211

CHAPTER 1
OUR FIRM CONVICTION

There are two things that we firmly believe in. The first is that a positive work culture, or a culture in which happiness at work is the focus, contributes to the wellbeing of employees and the success of organizations. The second belief is that you can only create such a culture by taking small steps and through experimentation. Then we met Rich Sheridan, Chief Storyteller at Menlo innovations. We held these two important beliefs for many years, but they were like loose puzzle pieces; we didn't know quite how to fit them into our workplaces or organizations. Then we met Rich Sheridan, Chief Storyteller at Menlo Innovations, and his talk helped us pop these puzzle pieces into place.

Sheridan—a tall, amiable, gray-haired man in his sixties—is one of the founders of Menlo Innovations. We met him at the International Happiness at Work Conference in Copenhagen. The night before he shared his story on stage, he told us about how his innovative IT company had a special mission: to "end human suffering in the world; as it relates to technology". A lofty goal for a 45-person company. But when Sheridan explains it, you understand and feel the intention. At Menlo they worked from the start to create a culture of joy for themselves, their clients, and the users of their software.

Menlo is not without their successes and accolades. In 2017, Menlo Innovations was listed in Forbes'[1] top 25 best companies[2]. Sheridan is understandably pleased with this accolade: "It indicates that we are a good example of how a culture can work for you." He even wrote a book about the subject and is now a popular speaker at international conferences about happiness at work and corporate culture, sharing examples from his own experiences of building this culture of joy at Menlo. "What is out of the ordinary for many organizations, is common for us. One of our most unusual practices is pair programming. Two people working on the same computer, doing the work of one, sounds like a crazy idea. In fact, it is far more productive. But I get a lot of raised eyebrows when I tell this. Another example: new parents are free to take their babies to work if they want to. During meetings you often see people with baby carriers holding their precious cargo, and for us this is a normal work scene. Our job interviews are done with 40 people at the same time. The applicants get all kinds of assignments that are not meant to put themselves into the spotlight, but are intended to help their fellow applicants make it to the next round." These are all unique examples of how a positive work culture can be incorporated in the practice of everyday work life.

How culture leads to success

At the end of the last century, management guru Peter Drucker famously said: "Culture eats strategy for breakfast." In other words, no matter how many good ideas you have, no matter how beautiful the strategy you outline, and no matter the great plans that you put down on paper, if the culture of the organization doesn't steer in the same direction, those plans won't work out. It's not just Menlo Innovations that knows how important corporate culture is for success. Companies like Johnson and Johnson, Southwest Airlines, technical service provider Guidion, and impact maker Tony's Chocolonely, all demonstrate that the careful construction and mainte-

---

1   Ahuja, Maneet & Burlingham, Bo (2020). '25 Companies That Believe Smaller is Better', Forbes. https://www.forbes.com/sites/maneetahuja/2020/05/12/forbes-small-giants-25-companies-that-believe-smaller-is-better/#4ca6b8821432. Consulted on 12 June 2020.

2   Category Small Businesses

nance of their corporate culture—one that is geared towards positivity—make it possible for them to flourish. That is the secret ingredient for their success, because it determines the biggest part of their competitive advantage. After all, anybody can copy everything that a company does except for its culture.

We were already aware that Menlo Innovations was a beautiful example of what a positive work culture looks like and the benefits that such a culture can yield. When Sheridan shared how his company continues to build upon its corporate structure, he confirmed our second belief: you cannot successfully develop a positive culture in one big step. Instead, many small steps are required. "How we have grown into what we are now, has not happened by following a strict plan. Just like in every other organization, things happen to us on a regular basis that we were not able to foresee. Developments in the market that mean a change of course or crazy ideas by colleagues which, once considered, may not be so crazy after all. My partner and I hear these ideas, then look at each other and say, 'Okay, we don't know what this will bring us, so let's run the experiment, then we'll find out.' This has now become Menlo's motto, and the open attitude that goes with it is one of the most important cultural values. The result is a unique corporate culture and a successful organization."

Run the experiment

While on the stage in Copenhagen, Sheridan shared one anecdote after another about how the team works at Menlo. When we heard the phrase run the experiment we looked at each other and grinned. "Run the experiment, that's it!" Extended culture-change programs with complex dependencies and detailed implementation plans that cover entire walls simply don't work. Changing via a stringent set of designs on paper is no longer how change happens, and maybe never worked in the first place. When people, teams and organizations want to change successfully, they first must let go of their ideas about changing in a structured way and according to a plan. There is another way that's so much better: get to work in short, clear steps. If you start creating a corporate culture on three different levels (individual, team, and organization), you will get much better results. This also means that it doesn't need to be perfect right away. There is no such thing as perfect. Don't try to invent all kinds of scenarios in advance; instead, approach your changes with the curiosity of a child. Culture change is a matter of getting started somewhere, anywhere. Then take small steps, try out new things on a small scale, and work out where to go next. What if something doesn't work? Then you simply adjust your idea. This work method also means that you do not push people into a change program from above or from outside, but that you invite them to participate and to change themselves from the inside out.

Once we had a grip on the principle of 'run the experiment' our puzzle was complete. Too often we hear that changing behavior and building a corporate culture is too difficult, too elusive, and too complicated to work. Which is a shame, because even though it does cost time, effort, and energy, it is also fun and rewarding. Building a positive work culture delivers a huge contribution to the end results, and to the success of you, your team, and your organization.

How to use this book?

In this book, just like in our training, education, and programs, we combine scientific research, handy models, examples, and exercises into a coherent method to change behavior on an individual, team, and organizational level. The Happy Office Manifesto is a practical guide to successfully change and build a corporate culture in which you and your colleagues can flourish, in any workplace. We show that happiness at work is not just a superficial or 'fluffy' thing. We also show you what you can do yourself to experience more joy in work and what your contribution is as a manager for your team's happiness at work. In addition, we explore how you can start creating a positive corporate culture on an organizational level. Throughout this book we use the word 'office' in a very broad sense. In other words, the contents of this book do not only apply to a traditional office setting, but to every work environment: from care to education, to construction and logistics, and from factory floor to working from home at the kitchen table. Would you like to get as much as possible out of it? Then grab a notebook to write down the results of the included exercises so you can immediately apply what you learn as you read. And even though you can do many things yourself when creating a positive work culture, it is much more fun to work together with your colleagues and your team, which will ultimately increase the end result and impact of your actions and interventions.

Finally

Finally, a remark for the observant reader. Even though 'run the experiment' is one of the basic principles of this book, there is no specific chapter dedicated to it. So, if you were looking for it, we are sorry to disappoint you. But we have a good reason. You cannot write a chapter, instruction, or a step-by-step plan for experimentation. You simply have to dive in and do it, in your own way, possibly with our help, and with examples of how we and others do that as a source of inspiration. You can find those examples throughout the book. We wish you much joy in reading it.

THE RELEVANCE OF HAPPINESS AT WORK AND A POSITIVE WORK CULTURE

Six months ago, account manager Marian got a new job. "I only now realize how important a positive atmosphere is in the workplace. In my previous job, my colleagues and I all worked on our own little islands. We did not ask each other for help, and we did not brainstorm about problems. There was never time for that. In hindsight, I realize that none of us actually knew how we contributed to the goals of the organization. I never felt that I, through my work, really made a difference. Of course, there were some colleagues that I got along with very well and we had fun together too, but there was also a lot of gossip going around. No, when I look back, I never got much energy from it. The organization where I work now couldn't be more different from my old situation. Here, everybody is truly interested in one another. At the beginning of the week, we discuss the goals as a team, and at the end of the week we all look at the results together. We share successes, express our appreciation and we give each other feedback. That ensures that I now have a lot more energy to go above and beyond with my work. In spite of all the stress and how busy we are, I now truly enjoy going to work."

Positive effects of happiness at work

Work plays an ever-increasing role in our lives, and over the past few years much research has been done regarding the more human aspects of work. We now know that people do their best work when they enjoy going to work. That people who are happy at their work are more flexible and can better deal with changes, stress, and workplace pressure. That they work better together, and are more innovative and productive. Happy people take fewer sick days, make fewer mistakes and have fewer accidents. If you look at all these positive effects of happiness at work, you would think that we would pay more attention to the topic and make choices that lead to a more positive work culture. And yet, even with all the evidence, we still don't see this in the majority of workplaces today.

> **The Business Case for Happiness at Work**
>
> Jessica Pryce Jones, an expert in psychology and happiness at work, did research in the US and UK about the difference between employees who were happy at work versus those who were unhappy[3]. The happiest employees turned out to be 47% more productive than the least happy group. Translated into days, that means an additional 1.25 days per week of productivity for people who were happy at work. Happy employees also took fewer sick days: on average a day and a half per year compared to six days for the least happy group. She also found that the energy levels of the happy people were much higher: a difference of 180% compared to the least happy group. Happy employees were 50% more motivated, experienced 28% more respect from their colleagues, and 31% more from their managers.
>
> Oswald, Proto, and Sgroi of the University of Warwick demonstrated in 2015 that people who

---

3   Pryce-Jones, Jessica (2010). Happiness at Work: Maximizing Your Psychological Capital for Success, Wiley.

> were happier were 12% more productive[4]. Shawn Achor, researcher in happiness at Harvard and author of The Happiness *Advantage*[5], mentions an increase in productivity of 31% and in turnover of 37%. Gallup[6] reports 17% higher productivity and 21% higher profitability. If you make the happiness of your employees a focal point of your organizational management, the benefits are clear. This doesn't mean that the research numbers will be exactly replicated in your organization; we cannot just assume that turnover and profit magically increase 21% if you start working towards having a positive culture. However, it's fair to assume that, based on these numbers, happy employees have a considerably higher positive effect on business operations than less happy employees, and that a positive work culture leads to better performances. It can also have a large positive effect in your organization. How much exactly? We cannot predict that. But what is certain, is that it does have an impact.

If you are familiar with these numbers, you would think that organizations would do everything in their power to facilitate happiness at work, that happiness in the workplace would be a widespread business model, and that a positive corporate culture would be a top priority for every management team. After all, the business operations and the results of the organization improve substantially when you start working on this. But we do not see this in organizations. We see that organizations recognize the importance of a positive culture and happiness at work, but they don't know where to start or how to go about getting it. They wrestle with how they should shape such a culture.

---

4   Oswald, Andrew J., Proto, Eugenio & Sgroi, Daniel (2015). 'Happiness and productivity', Journal of Labor Economics, 33 (4), pp. 789-822.

5   Achor, Shawn (2011). The Happiness advantage.

6   Gallup (2017). State of the Global Workplace (rapport). Consulted on 21 January 2020.

Working in the 21st century

Over the years, much has changed in the way we think about work. From focusing on increasing production by using machines to efficiency improvements by means of time management. From 'getting things done' to increased focus on the individual and their needs and talents. From 'how can it be done faster' to 'how can it be done better, more effectively and faster'. We have discovered that there is a limit to productivity, to time management, and to standardization of needs. In this new age we have also seen an increase in stress-related illnesses. More voices are calling for a change of direction and in more organizations the focus is being redirected to happiness at work and a positive work culture. It has also become clear that the time has come where we really must look at what people need to flourish. This starts with understanding the 'threats' to wellbeing present in the 21st century workplace and with understanding our own lens through which we view the world.

The world around us changes faster than ever

As we enter the third decade of the 21st century, pressure in the workplace is at an all-time high. Everything must be done fast, faster—should have been done yesterday. We can barely catch our breath after one change before we must get ready for the next one. Never before have things moved as quickly as they do now; what seemed like a promising business model last year is outdated this year. The life cycle of organizations is shorter than it has ever been. We are asked to work more efficiently and effectively because profits must go up every year, increasing the pressure to perform. Influenced by all these factors, large groups of people don't feel comfortable at work. People were not designed for this continuous change and pressure to perform. It frustrates them, leading to disengagement, exhaustion and burnout. The number of people reporting burnout in the Netherlands is sky high. In the course of ten years, according to research by the TNO[7], the number of people with complaining of burnout has risen from over 11 to 16%. The most commonly reported causes of these complaints were decreased autonomy and higher demands, and

---

7   TNO (2019). Arbobalans 2019 (rapport).

these numbers date back to before the COVID-19 pandemic.

In her book The Burnout Epidemic, Jennifer Moss reports that "Burnout is a global problem". Her research found burnout and its causes in more than 46 countries.

Worldwide research by Indeed[8] conducted in 2021 showed that the number of people experiencing burnout is growing. More than half of workers said they felt burned out and more than two-thirds said the feeling had gotten worse throughout the pandemic.

> **Technological Changes**
>
> Technology has made our lives easier in many areas; while we're no longer able to imagine our work without computers, email or internet, the current technology explosion has also had negative consequences, such as information overload and an addiction to social media. These all result in a loss of concentration, depth, and focus, and all these technological developments decrease our face-to-face communication. According to research, when our desks are more than 30 feet from one another we prefer to send an email rather than asking the question in person. Some people also report feeling insecure about the enormous amounts of technological changes. Do they have sufficient knowledge and experience to keep pace? In 2018, the World Economic Forum predicted that 52% of all the work would be done by robots in 2025, compared to 29 percent in 2018. Will your job still exist in the (near) future, or will a robot take over from you?

---

8   https://www.cnbc.com/2021/09/23/the-future-of-work-is-here-employee-burnout-needs-to-go.html

How our view of the world has changed

As a result of living through constant change (not to mention threats to our health, job security and livelihoods), our perception of what is normal or desirable has changed as well. Organizations that adapt to these shifts have an opportunity to increase happiness in the workplace. In some organizations these shifts have already taken place, while in other organizations this is still quite a long way off (or it doesn't fit into their current view of reality at all). These shifts are:

A. From Control to Trust

Sometimes people say: trust is good, control is better. But in real life it usually turns out to be the other way around: control is good, trust is better. When we start with trust, employees get more autonomy, the hierarchy decreases, and employees assume more responsibility and ownership. We talk less about "I have a right to" and more about "how can I contribute?". We don't say "that is not in my job description" but "how can we achieve this together?". There is a growing group of people who indicate that they believe that people are naturally inclined to do the right thing, that people can be trusted.

B. From Profit Driven to Purpose Driven Work

More and more people and organizations recognize that having a purpose is more important than profit. Who loves to go to work to make more profit for the shareholders? People would rather get out of bed for something that they consider worthwhile, that means something, that makes the world or their own living environment a little better, or where they can mean something for other people.

C. From Managing to Leading

Successful leaders of the future have self-awareness, understand that a personal and people-oriented approach is the only way, and would rather stimulate change, behavior, and culture in order to achieve results together. Their own happiness at work and that of their employees is thereby a leading factor, a necessary precondition.

> **Chicken or the Egg?**
>
> An important question in response to research into happiness (at work) is whether happiness leads to better performance or if better performance leads to more happiness. It appears to work both ways. Most research indicates that happiness leads to better performance, and that better performance, to a lesser degree, also leads to happiness.

What do people and organizations need?

How can we face the challenges of our times? The key doesn't lie in smarter technology, greater knowledge, or working even more efficiently but in focusing on employees and organizational culture. Organizations will struggle to distinguish themselves through products or services alone. Most companies' products can be picked up from other companies, and technology is accessible for almost everyone. What cannot be copied, and is unique in every organization, is the system, the way of cooperating, how employees behave towards each other; in other words, the organizational culture.

> **THE KEY TO SUCCESS IN THE FUTURE LIES IN EMPLOYEES AND ORGANIZATIONAL CULTURE.**

Organizations need flexible, involved, resilient, and creative employees. Employees who take ownership, who assume responsibility not just for their own situation but for the success of their colleagues and the overall success of the business. If we look at what people need, we find that organizations play an important role in the fulfillment of the psychological basic human needs of: comptence, autonomy, and relatedness[9][10]. People function at their best when they can chart their own course, when they experience a certain level of autonomy. When people feel that they are controlled, micromanaged or under too much pressure, their performance is impacted. Relatedness is about a feeling of belonging, having social contacts, and having relationships at work, with colleagues, managers, and clients. In other words, the feeling that you matter. People also feel the need to do things that they are good at, to employ their talents and to make a difference because of it. When these needs are met, employees feel good about themselves, are intrinsically motivated, perform better, and are happier at work.

Work is also valuable for people in a psychological sense. There are many reasons why people go to work[11]. For some people, their work is a part of life and is something that needs to be done. For others it is their position in society that counts. For most there is the obvious fact that money needs to be earned in order to live; work makes us feel useful and gives us a sense of fulfillment as human beings. There are many more benefits to work; it can give you satisfaction if you can learn from it, if you can do new things, if you can develop yourself, if you can do what you think is important. Many people just think of work as 'being fun'. The basic needs of human beings are fulfilled in different ways by their job. It is important

---

9   Ryan, Richard & Deci, Edward (2000). 'Self-Determination Theory and the Facilitation of Intrinsic Motivation, Social Development, and Well-Being', American Psychologist, 55 (1), pp. 68-78.

10   Broeck, Anja Van den, et al. (2016). 'A Review of Self-Determination Theory's Basic Psychological Needs at Work', Journal of Management, 42 (5), pp. 1195-1229.

11   McGregor, Lindsay & Doshi, Neel (2015). 'How Company Culture Shapes Employee Motivation', Harvard Business Review. https://hbr.org/2015/11/how-company-culture-shapes-employee-motivation. Consulted on May 1, 2020. Jennifer Moss, 'The Burnout Epidemic

for organizations, if they wish to focus on happiness at work and a positive work culture, to understand these basic needs and to know how they can implement them in the workplace.

CHAPTER 2

THE TRUTHS AND MYTHS OF HAPPINESS AT WORK

Atmosphere at work is important for many people, and project manager James is no exception to this. He told us that, as far as he is concerned, a constructive discussion only works well if everybody is open to it and is not afraid to express themselves. He believes that happiness at work is one of the conditions for this. "If my colleague and I feel comfortable and happy in the team, everything already runs more smoothly. The threshold to start (difficult?) discussions is lower, we help each other, and we can solve problems. In our case happiness at work is a subject that we discuss at every team meeting. We have talked about what makes us happy and how we can improve it. It was nice to discover that different things make different people happy but there is also a lot of overlap. That's where we put our primary focus," he says. James is correct: happiness means different things to different people. Before we can get to work with happiness at work and make it practical, we must first be clear: what exactly does Happiness at Work mean?

WHAT IS HAPPINESS AT WORK?

Let's cut to the chase: there is no single all-encompassing definition of happiness at work. It is subjective: what makes one person happy can mean deep distress for another person. Many scientists and authors have delved into the subject during the past few years, libraries full of books have been written on it. Despite all the attention we still believe that one of our clients gave us the best definition of all: happiness at work is to whistle on your way to work and to whistle on your way back home.

As far as we're concerned, this metaphor describes exactly what it's all about: experiencing positive emotions, looking forward to your day, feeling energetic, fit, and resilient, being ready to meet the challenges of the day—and when going back home, still feeling energized. You could be tired after a full day of work, but at least you feel good about your results and what you have achieved together with your colleagues. Proud and satisfied about the steps you have taken towards a useful and deserving goal, but not so tired or exhausted that you no longer have the energy to play with your kids at night or enjoy whatever hobbies you pursue outside of your work life. In short, happiness at work is about short-term enjoyment and about the deeper feelings of satisfaction, connection, and meaning that you can experience through your work.

> **Annie**: "So, You're telling me that when I am happy at work, I will be whistling on my way there and on my way home, every single day? That seems exaggerated to me."

> Of course, it is not realistic to go to and from work whistling every day. There are bound to be days where you just don't feel like it. Rainy days, days when you're stuck in traffic, when your weekend was just too great to go back to work on Monday. Working towards happiness at work will not eliminate those moments. It is not a magic potion. Work doesn't need to be fun all the time. Not all feedback needs to be positive, and not all problems need to be referred to as 'challenges'. It is natural to have a lousy day every now and then.

Happiness is not as much about the absence of unhappiness and of negative feelings such as sadness, frustration, or insecurity but more about the ability to deal with them.

A Couple of Definitions of Happiness at Work

The increasing interest in this subject has led to many different definitions.

Shawn Achor, author of Happiness Advantage, refers to happiness as 'the joy you feel growing towards your potential.'

Jessica Pryce-Jones gives us a definition in her book Happiness at Work that appeals very much to us: 'Happiness at work is a mindset which allows you to maximize performance and achieve your potential by being aware of the highs and lows in your work. Happiness at work is an approach, a method, and it doesn't just concern yourself but rather what you do together with others.'

What we find interesting about this definition is the fact that both negative and positive emotions are included here. Positive emotions are important, of course. However, negative experiences, being out of your comfort zone, working very hard for something that you consider important, and stretching yourself as far as you can go, these are the things that make us happy in the long run.

Alexander Kjerulf, *author of several books about happiness at work and founder of the international cho network The Woohoo Partnership*, simply refers to happiness at work as: 'The feeling of happiness you get at work.' Simple and

> *effective; everybody can remember this definition.*

WHAT IS THE ROLE OF EMOTIONS?

Happiness at work is about regularly experiencing both positive and negative emotions. What are those emotions, how do they affect us and why are they relevant at work?

Broaden & build theory

Our emotions determine in a large part how we function and how we perform. Barbara Fredrickson, professor of Psychology at the University of North Carolina, has been working on her Broaden & Build theory for 20 years.
Summarized, this theory is about how experiencing positive emotions ensures that you open yourself up more (broaden) and are prepared to try new things. Positive emotions also provide for growth (build), better cooperation, and more tolerance with respect to other people. Of course, this only counts for truly felt emotions, no fake-it-till-you-make-it-positivity. By experiencing real emotions, we create a bond with other people and that increases our chances for survival in the long run.

> **Annie:** *"I heard there are studies that say that you actually should fake it, with smiling and such, and that you will then truly experience the positive emotions?"*

There are people who claim that you should start every day with a smile and that everything will be alright. Have you ever tried that? Well, we tried it ourselves, and we know now that, for us at least, this doesn't work. Putting on a fake smile in the morning did not make us one bit happier. Science supports this: there is research that shows that suppressing your negative emotions and acting as if you are positive is bad for you, increasing your blood pressure and your heart rate. People around you feel it when something is fake, and it tends to make them uneasy. So no, pretending doesn't work. That doesn't mean that you should just wallow in nega-

tivity. Sometimes you could try to focus more on feeling better or using more positive language. In the end that makes your life more enjoyable; for yourself and for those around you.

More positive emotions than negative ones

In order to flourish, perform and experience happiness at work, it is important that you experience positive emotions. But life is not just fun and games. There are things that are less pleasant, which cause us to experience negative emotions. Negative emotions impact us more, we experience them with more intensity, and we also remember them longer. Psychologists refer to that as the negativity bias. That's why we need more positive emotions than negative ones to achieve a good balance. In other words: for every moment of frustration that we experience, we should aim to balance that with more moments of satisfaction or fun.

> ### 🏋 Exercise
> How many positive and negative emotions do you experience in a day? Keep track of them and look at the causes too. By doing this consciously, you may find that you start noticing positive emotions more.

Fight, flight, freeze versus the neocortex

Where positive emotions provide for a widening of our view, negative emotions make it narrower. Fear, frustration, and anger demand all of our brain's capacity and bring us into the fight-flight-freeze mode of our reptilian brain. This mode ensures that we are 100% ready for the danger we are anticipating. This is great because it helps us react quickly if we need to jump out of the way of an approaching car. Our neocortex, the part of our brain that we use to think actively and to make plans, will be turned off at that moment. In this instance, it's not a good idea to come up with a strategy or to think about jumping out of the way. That would take much too long. Our reptilian brain helps us to survive in the short term when faced with perceived immediate threats. But it is also possible that if the situation is not instant death it gets in our way, because our reptilian brain means we can not see opportunities, chances, and solutions. The minute a colleague makes a remark that feels like a personal attack, our reptilian brain jumps into action. We then react instinctively, jump into the fight-flight-freeze mode which makes it harder to see the remark from the right perspective. Once we have leapt into this way of thinking it is difficult to get out; to turn our neocortex back on. It can be helpful to think about the question: is what I see, think, and feel actually true?

Negative emotions are helpful with change

Emotions such as fear, frustration, and anger have more to offer: they can trigger change. If we feel good, we are less motivated to change or improve things. It is the periods of unhappiness that lead to more self-knowledge, resilience, and vigor. You could regard frustration and anger as something positive. Where there is frustration, there is energy that you can use to get to business, for yourself or for your team. Go ahead and celebrate that frustration!

Getting to know your emotions

Recognizing your emotions is very important. The better you know your emotions, both negative and positive, the stronger and more resilient you become. Psychologists refer to that as 'emotional diversity'. Author Mark Manson compares this with a stock portfolio: diversification is good![12] A more diverse portfolio yields less risk. The same goes for our emotional life. By knowing our emotions better—both the negative and the positive—and recognising their impact, we learn how to better deal with them.

> **Exercise**
>
> On average, Dutch people have 1.1 bad days at work every week, compared to 3.6 good days. Do you feel the same? How many bad days at work do you have

---

12   Manson, Mark (2017). 'Happiness Is Not Enough', Markmanson.net. https://markmanson.net/happiness-is-not-enough. Consulted on April 23, 2020.

> per week on average, where negative feelings are most prominent? What causes that? How do you deal with it if you have a bad day? What proportion of bad days is acceptable for you? What about if your colleague has a bad day? How do you deal with that?

THE DIFFERENCE BETWEEN HAPPINESS AT WORK AND JOB SATISFACTION

One of our clients, a manager at a law firm, once desperately told us: "I just don't understand. We give our employees everything: a big salary, a fancy company car, fresh fruit, a membership for the gym. We have a beautiful office, we cater an extensive luncheon every day and still they complain." We asked her how people dealt with each other at the office, what the general view was about the division of work, the rewards, promotions, the atmosphere, and what the gossip at the watercooler was about. This quickly revealed that there was a lot of room for improvement. The company did want their people to be happy, but they used the wrong approach. All their interventions and efforts for improvement contributed to job satisfaction and not to the factors that lead to happiness at work. Even though the intentions were good, all those investments did not lead to the desired effect.

Thinking versus experiencing

When you start working on happiness at work, it is important to realize the difference between happiness at work and job satisfaction. This difference is based on the work of Daniel Kahneman, the Israeli psychologist who received the Nobel prize for Economic Sciences in 2002 for his work about how we think and make decisions. In his book Thinking Fast and Slow, Kahneman describes two ways of thinking:

1. Fast thinking, based on previous experiences, feelings, and associations
2. Slow thinking, logical, and reasoned.

If we apply this theory to work, that brings us to the difference between happiness at work and job satisfaction[13]. Happiness at work (experienced wellbeing) is about experiencing positive emotions, wellbeing, feeling good right now. Job satisfaction (evaluated wellbeing) in contrast, is about how you think about your wellbeing. These two are related but are essentially different concepts and they have different influencers (input) and results (output). The input for job satisfaction is mostly about things such as salary, promotion, free fruit, and a membership to a gym. In many employee engagement studies, it is mostly this component that is examined. Happiness at work arises from different aspects: this is more about experiencing joy and fulfilment at the end of the day, making progress, having nice colleagues that you can have fun with, and working in an environment in which you feel safe, where you are allowed to make mistakes, and where you can do meaningful work. These are aspects that shape how you experience your work. The situation in the rest of your life also has an influence. How are things at home, with your family, your health, and your relationship? Happiness at work is in your heart, job satisfaction is in your head.

Difference in output

Happiness at work and job satisfaction also have different outcomes. The output of job satisfaction is mostly the answer to the question: do I want to continue working here? Suppose that there are two organizations where everything is the same, the same atmosphere and the same work, but at one organization you can earn more money, then it is reasonable that you opt for the job with the higher salary. But suppose that in one organization your work is more useful, you receive more appreciation, and people interact more joyfully. Surely that would make a higher salary at an organization where the atmosphere isn't as good a less attractive option. Wouldn't it?

The outputs of happiness at work are all about performance. Happy people perform better, on a lot of different levels. They are more creative and more productive, they work better

---

13   Kjerulf, Alexander (2016). Kahneman's Hybrid Model of Happiness, Woohoo Academy.

together, are more involved and inspired. And this is exactly what the manager of the law firm was looking for. She wanted more engagement and enthusiasm. What she wanted was a happy workforce, but what she did only created more job satisfaction. Together we looked at how she could facilitate happiness at work in the firm, with a significantly better result.

The relationship between happiness at work and job satisfaction

Happiness at work and job satisfaction are related and influence each other. However, it turns out that the influence of happiness at work on job satisfaction is many times greater than the other way around. If we are happy at work, that also makes us more satisfied. If we are satisfied at work, that only makes us a little bit happier.

So, the factors that lead to job satisfaction indirectly influence happiness at work—except when they are not good, then they influence our happiness at work in a negative way. Factors such as salary, the office, technology (equipment and systems

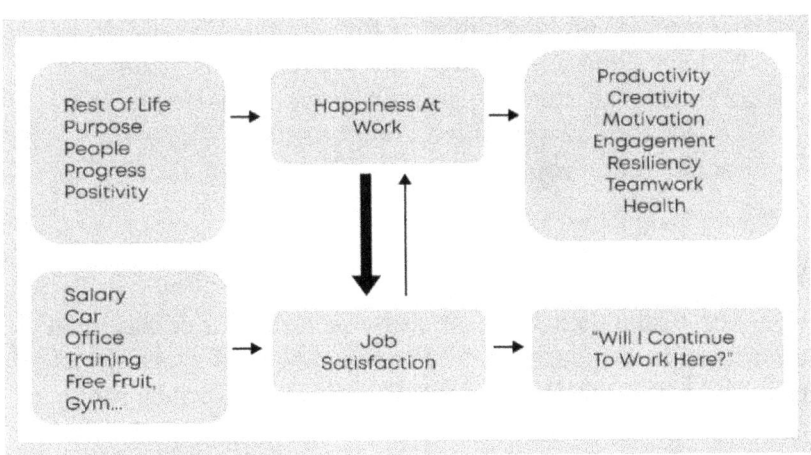

Kaheman's Hybrid Model of Happiness - A. Kjerulf

access) and the company restaurant influence our happiness at work in a negative way when they are not fair or if they have been taken away. Say for instance that you feel that your salary is not fair compared to your colleague or you have to wait 15 minutes every day before your computer has started up, then that comes at the expense of your happiness at work. As an organization, you must make sure that these basics are taken care of. The same goes for communication: if the leadership of an organization is unclear about vision and strategy, if the communication is deficient, then that makes us angry and unhappy. However, if the communication is clear, we just consider that to be normal. Best case scenario, we're content; worst case scenario, we're unhappy.

> **Annie:** "So, money doesn't make you happy at all?"

Money by itself doesn't make you happy—it's just metal or paper or a number in your bank app—but the opportunities that money offers can make you happy. The fact that we earn money and support our families is certainly something to be proud of. We don't want to trivialize the importance of money; it offers feelings of freedom, security, and the possibility to choose what we want to do with our lives—but there is a limit. Research shows that once a yearly salary of approximately US$70,000 US dollars has been reached, a salary increase does not contribute substantially to more happiness. However if you lack money or you are compensated unfairly, then that can make you extremely unhappy.

Why salary doesn't contribute to happiness

Why don't salaries, fresh fruit and a beautiful office essentially contribute to our happiness? There are two reasons behind this. The first is 'hedonic adaptation', a psychological term relating to how humans eventually become insensitive to new stimuli and settle into a new emotional baseline - we 'get used to it'.. A raise in salary feels great, of course, but after a few weeks that higher salary becomes your 'new normal'. It doesn't really make you happy anymore. It does not yield more positive emotions. The second reason is that job benefits and salary invite comparison. Say you get a salary increase of $500—that makes you feel happy. But the next day you discover that your colleague, who (from your perspective) performs exactly the same tasks, received an increase of $1,000. Your happiness evaporates immediately. This unfairness (perceived or real) makes most people even less happy than they were before the salary increase.

The spoiling trap

Many organizations that start working on happiness at work make the common mistake in attempting to design the so-called 'employee experience'. They 'spoil' their employees by providing all kinds of things for them – fresh fruit, dry cleaning service, bigger, more beautiful cars – and they overdo it. "People don't realize how good they have it here," is what we often hear. A client told us once: "Sometimes I just wanted to institute Siberian weeks here. With a regular Mr. Coffee instead of the luxurious espresso machine. And have them bring a brownbag lunch from home instead of providing a fully catered lunch. Who knows, maybe then they'd appreciate it again…" Unfortunately, that would not lead to the desired result because the espresso machine and the catered luncheon have become standard. Once you have such provisions people quickly come to feel they're entitled to them, and taking things away from people truly hurts. Look before you leap when it comes to perks and office design, and if you really must withdraw any employee benefits, be sure to explain your reasons clearly.

Where to focus?

When we explain to clients what the difference is between happiness at work and job satisfaction, that almost always leads to an 'aha' moment. Because suddenly it becomes very clear where the focus should be, namely on the factors that contribute to happiness at work. Once you understand this, you can start to consider how those aspects that initially lead to job satisfaction also can be utilized to increase happiness at work. For instance, that coffee machine could be a meeting place for colleagues to get to know each other better. The membership for a gym could lead to colleagues working out together. That way you work on better work relationships, leading to an increase in happiness at work.

> **Annie:** *"Well, uh, that great cup of coffee in the morning does truly make me very happy, you know."*
>
> *Of course you like your morning coffee! So do we! But is that really happiness? We do not think so. Suppose that for one or another reason or another, we could no longer drink coffee. Would that really make us less happy? It wouldn't. Happiness is about connection with others, about results, about the things we mentioned before. Once you become accustomed to a morning tea, you would be equally happy. That doesn't mean that you cannot tremendously enjoy that cup of coffee every day.*

WHAT CAUSES UNHAPPINESS AT WORK?

Research[14] that we carried out in 2021, in conjunction with MonitorGroep and Gelukkig Werken Nederland, shows that there are many factors that impede happiness at work. According to the respondents, the number one cause of unhappiness at work is high work pressure. When people experience too much pressure at work it causes stress which increasingly expresses itself in health problems.

According to our 2021 research, 48% of Dutch people experienced high work pressure—however 31% of respondents felt that work pressure didn't bother them. 'Buzzing at work' gave them a lot of satisfaction and enjoyment. However, our study also showed that 17% of people suffered from excessively high work pressures, making their happiness at work considerably lower than that of the first group. It is a fine line between 'buzzing' and 'too busy'. We are by no means advocating for laziness in the workplace; work pressure that is too low is also a reason for unhappiness[15].

---

14   Monitor Groep (2021). Nationaal Werkgeluk Onderzoek 2021.
15   Ibid

> **There is No Such Thing as Work Pressure**
>
> In 2018 the costs related to absence because of stress at work in the Netherlands was as much as 2.8 billion Euros, according to the calculations of tno. Therefore, stress and pressure at work are themes that we must take seriously, and organizations must tackle them. At the same time, it is important to keep perspective. Work pressure is not tangible; you cannot measure it. What feels like pressure for one person is no big deal for someone else. Also, stress, sadness, and fear in the short term don't necessarily mean that we are unhappy in the long run. It has a lot to do with how we perceive pressure at work, who we are as people, what is happening in our outside world, and our personality and communication preferences. Our research also showed that employees themselves are an important cause of pressure at work with our survey showing responses such as: "I'm going for the highest possible quality." I have a hard time saying 'no'."

MYTHS ABOUT HAPPINESS AT WORK: WHAT IS TRUE?

Myth 1: Happiness at Work is Superficial Hype

With the increasing attention on happiness at work we start to encounter criticism of the movement. The most common point of critique is that happiness at work is 'superficial and commercial hype'. Some people think that working on happiness at work means that you must always be positive and happy—which, understandably, puts people's backs up. In one company we actually heard someone say that he was 'against happiness at work'. When we asked for clarification it turned out that he meant the superficial Facebook and Instagram happiness, or toxic positivity. The image that the media draws about ball pits, yoga at the office, and other hyped up office gadgets doesn't help the mission. We also run the risk that a superficial approach to happiness at work over-inflates our expectations of how happy, successful, and appreciated we should feel every day. If our work isn't fun for just a moment, we are disappointed and we can even have feelings of failure. The outcomes of this warped view of happiness at work can go on to cause an inability to handle negativity well. Negative emotions are a part of life, and they have an important function.

Myth 2: Happiness at Work is a Goal in Itself

Can you strive for happiness, and is that something we should want? In reality, happiness is not a permanent state of being. It fluctuates under the influence of our actions. As Johan Cruyff said: 'To be happy you must do things that make you happy.' Sometimes that works, and other times it doesn't. It's not just a tick box on a to-do list that you can check off. Happiness comes and goes and sometimes you don't notice it until it's gone. The art is in learning to recognize and be aware of happiness. This means that, in any role, it is you who is primarily responsible for your happiness at work.

Myth 3: Happiness is the Absence of Unhappiness

People look at the world in different ways and that means that some people have a more pessimistic view of the world than others. A part of them assumes that life brings mostly misfortune—if you always assume the worst, it feels good when things turn out better than expected. In a way, there doesn't seem to be a disadvantage to having such a pessimistic view, however this attitude to life will not lead to large changes, special performances, or a feeling of happiness. Taking away and stopping things that make us unhappy leads to mediocrity at best—in the end that doesn't make anybody happy.

Myth 4: The Ultimate Focus on Happiness at Work, That's What It's All About

We regard it as our mission to normalize happiness at work in organizations. We ask attention for it, and we hope that organizations make it a point of discussion. But... that comes with a risk. Research shows that 'focusing too much on happiness' can make you unhappy. This study is a follow up on earlier research where students were shown a comical movie or a sad movie just before they had to do a math assignment. It turned out that the ones who had watched the comedy scored better than the ones who had watched the sad movie. In the new research they tried something else. Now the whole group was shown a comedy, but half of the participants were given an article to read in which the importance of being happy was emphasized. The other half received no reading material. After the movie all test subjects were questioned about how happy they felt. The group who had read the article felt less happy. Conclusion? If happiness becomes a 'must', it no longer works. So, making happiness at work a performance indicator and trying to build programs and processes around increasing happiness can lead to the opposite effect. Talking too much about it and even measuring happiness at work can contribute to this negative effect. For some people, being asked every day or every week 'how happy are you?' can decrease their happiness.

Myth 5: Happiness at Work is the Same as Engagement

In workplaces there is often some confusion about the relationship between engagement and happiness at work. Organizations talk about employee engagement, which refers to the involvement of employees, how engaged or committed they are. It is about the relationship that an employee has with an employer, how involved someone feels with the organization. Work engagement refers to involvement with the work itself, an employee's enthusiasm about their job. Happiness at work is a broader concept. We know people who were very engaged and committed to their job but still not happy at work. They did not feel a connection with their employer or their colleagues, and they quickly accepted better offers elsewhere. The opposite can also be found; people who are very committed to the goal of the organization but who cannot get excited about the actual work anymore. Happiness at work encompasses aspects such as job satisfaction, enthusiasm, involvement, and wellbeing, and it is both the cause and the result of success. By just focusing on engagement instead of on happiness at work we shortchange ourselves as employees and as organizations. What would you rather be, happy or engaged?

CHAPTER 3

THE PILLARS OF HAPPINESS AT WORK: 4 P'S

How do you create more happiness at work and a positive work culture? Things that make you happy could make your colleague very unhappy. What works in one team could very well be completely off base in the other team. There is no such thing as a 'one size fits all' approach. The good news is there are many similarities in what makes people happy at work. When we ask participants in our workshops and training sessions to discuss their best work experiences, certain common elements emerge. These map to what science tells us about happiness at work. Try it for yourself with the following exercise:

> **🏋 Exercise: Best Work Experience**
>
> Think about the best work experience you have ever had, one that truly made you happy. Be as specific as possible.
>
> What was it? Where, when, and with whom did it happen? Why did this experience make you so happy? What was it that you felt at the time? Then think about what contributed most to your best work experience.

Was Your Best Work Experience About:

1. A promotion? - yes / no
2. Receiving your monthly salary? - yes / no
3. An increase in salary? - yes / no
4. A beautiful office environment? - yes / no
5. Having fun with your colleagues? - yes / no
6. Achieving a result that was important for you? - yes / no
7. Doing something for someone else? - yes / no
8. Something you did together with other people? - yes / no
9. Something that gave you much enjoyment? - yes / no
10. A show of appreciation from others, acknowledging that you had done a good job? - yes / no

Now make a list of the five most important things that contribute to your happiness at work.

Annie: *"How does the exercise 'best work experience' contribute to happiness at work?"*

Thinking about your best work experience makes you happy because the memory of this experience evokes positive emotions. You get to experience that happy feeling all over again. Try asking someone else to do this exercise with you. This can be even more powerful, because we experience happiness when we see others enjoy reliving their best work experience. Our response is caused by our mirror neurons: When someone shares a story with us about something that makes them truly happy, mirror neurons allow us to share a little bit of that feeling too.

FOUR FACTORS THAT MAKE US HAPPY

During our training sessions, we've never met a single person who described their best work experience as the moment when they looked at their bank account and were happy to see that their salary had been deposited. It has also never been about a free apple or pear, a beautiful car, or a pension fund. When we ask participants what makes them happy at work, they describe times when they provided a meaningful experience or service for another person. Moments of satisfaction, development and growth, or moments when they felt connected and had fun with their colleagues. These stories are only partially to do with the work environment, organizational processes and structures, and even less to do with reward systems and work benefits.

If we look at science, and our own exprienes, then we can summarize what is really important for people into four factors:

1. Purpose
2. People
3. Progress
4. Positivity

PURPOSE

PEOPLE

POSITIVITY

PROGRESS

We call these the four pillars of happiness at work. These four pillars—the four Ps—are closely connected, and overlap with one another. Purpose is about being aware of why you do what you do, and leads to a feeling of meaning.

People means that your colleagues matter to you and that you feel connected to them. Progress is about experiencing progress in your work and in your own development, which leads to satisfaction. Positivity is about an optimistic mindset, feeling good in your own skin and having fun. Each of these pillars is important at different levels, for yourself, your team, and the organization.

PILLAR 1: PURPOSE

Greek philosophers Aristotle and Epicurus knew back in around 300 BC—and modern science confirms this—that doing meaningful work is important for a person's levels of happiness at work. Nine out of ten people are prepared to accept lower wages if they get to do work that is meaningful to them[16]. Purpose is about contributing to something bigger than yourself. How do you make a difference for someone else? Is what you do useful, does it make sense? There is nothing more demotivating than finishing a project and seeing the result of your efforts consigned to the bottom of a drawer or tossed into a wastebasket.

An experiment[17] where people were asked to build dolls from LEGO shows how our motivation is connected to purpose. The participants were split into two groups. In the first group, after completing the task, the dolls were disassembled right in front of their eyes. In the second group, the researcher displayed all the built dolls prominently in a row and praised the participants for their work. Unsurprisingly, the first group gave up on the task a lot quicker than the second. Having clarity on why you do what you do and being acknowledged for your efforts is very important for our motivation. When we dive deeper into the concept of 'purpose', we see it is a very comprehensive subject. Personal purpose for an individual, for instance, is not the same as the purpose of a team or an organization. However, when someone's personal purpose can be connected to that of the team and/or organization, this reinforces a feeling of connection to our purpose.

Organizational purpose

When we look at organizational purpose[18], we define this as:

---

16   Achor, Shawn, et al. (2018). '9 Out of 10 People Are Willing to Earn Less Money to Do More-Meaningful Work', Harvard Business Review. https://hbr.og/2018/11/9-out-of-10-people-are-willing-to-earn-less-money-to-do-more-meaningful-work. Consulted on May 6, 2020.

17   Pink, Daniel H. (2010) Drive. De verrassende waarheid over wat ons motiveert, Business Contact. Translated by Vanja Walsmit.

18   Beacon Institute (n.d.). EY – Building a better working world. https://www.ey.com/gl/en/issues/ey-beacon-institute-the-business-case-for-purpose. Consulted on May 15, 2020.

"an ambitious reason for being in business. One that inspires employees and those involved to take action and that benefits the local or global community". Having organizational purpose and acting in accordance with it not only contributes to the happiness of employees, but it is also good for business results. Ernst & Young's worldwide research on the importance of organizational purpose for managers found that of the 474 managers interviewed, 94% acknowledged the importance of a purpose, but only 46% indicated that they actually used the purpose when making strategic and operational decisions. This is a missed opportunity for these organizations, because it turns out that having a strong organizational purpose has a significant effect on business outcomes[19]. Organizations where purpose is felt strongly, show better financial results when compared to their competitors, better organizational culture, and higher satisfaction of both employees and clients than organizations where the purpose is only felt slightly or not at all.

> **Purpose is Not the Same as Vision, Mission, and Targets**
>
> We regularly hear people wondering what the difference is between purpose, vision, mission, and targets. There are many schools of thought on the differences between these concepts. In the context of this book we use the following definitions:
>
> **Purpose** is the need to have impact. To mean something to someone else.
>
> **Mission** is the strategy to achieve that purpose. With **Vision** we indicate what the world looks like when our purpose has been fulfilled.
>
> **Targets** are the smaller, easier, achievable steps on the road to the purpose.

---

19   Deloitte (2013). 2013: Culture of purpose. https://www2.deloitte.com/us/en/pages/about-deloitte/articles/culture-of-purpose.html. Consulted on May15, 2020.

Personal purpose

Your personal purpose at work is about how you as an individual can contribute positively to the organization or environment that you are part of. Consider the purpose pyramid[20]: people who can contribute to something larger than themselves experience personal purpose at work on all three levels of the pyramid.

THE PURPOSE PYRAMID

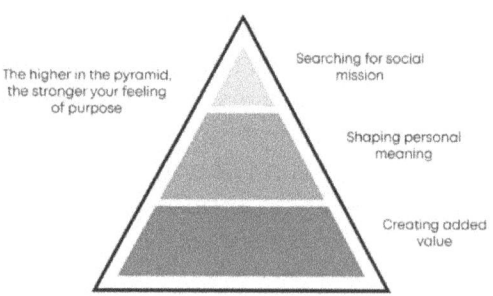

The higher in the pyramid, the stronger your feeling of purpose

- Searching for social mission
- Shaping personal meaning
- Creating added value

Level 1. Create added value (without doing harm to others)

We start at the base of the purpose pyramid: The first level is about the value that your work represents for others within or outside of your organization. For instance, an employee in payroll who makes sure that their colleagues receive their salary on time every month. Or, when you sell products to a client, the contribution those products make to the revenue and growth of an organization. Generating income for your family can give you a sense of purpose. Therefore, the simple act of working contributes to a sense of meaning. Not only does it make us feel that we are part of the community, but it also gives us social and community standing, and the fact that we earn money by doing it makes us feel useful. Mind you, when your work has adverse effects for others, this diminishes your feeling of meaning. For example, if you are a buyer and you pay your suppliers such a low price that they can barely

---

20   Hansen, Morten (2018). Great at Work: How Top Performers Do Less, Work Better, and Achieve More, Simon & Schuster.

exist. Even though this contributes to the revenue and profit of your organization, it has explicitly adverse consequences for another group. We often see that people experience this first level of the purpose pyramid in their work, but fail to think about improving on their purpose. That is a shame, because it is at the second level that you look at what your work means to you personally.

Level 2. Shape personal meaning

The middle level of the purpose pyramid is about the personal meaning of your work. This is where you connect what you like to do with what you think is important and what you are good at—in other words, your purpose. By making a personal connection the difference that you make for others becomes more meaningful. For example, if you are a cleaner in a hospital you might reflect on how your work contributes to the health of patients, and you notice that you can contribute even more by talking to patients while you're cleaning. You can only reach this second level when the first level has been achieved, and the higher you climb on the pyramid, the stronger your connection with your purpose.

Level 3. Searching for a social mission

If you want to reach the highest level of the purpose pyramid, then it is important that the organization where you work also has a social mission, and that you understand that mission and how you contribute to it. Only a small percentage of working people experience this level of purpose in their work (17%). Working with this kind of purpose causes people to be very driven and inspired. Contributing to a social mission gives energy and focus, and ensures that more gets accomplished. The only problem is that not every organization will have a social mission, or they have one that is poorly defined.

Bullshit Jobs

David Graeber[21] is a student of the phenomenon of 'useless work'. In 2013, he wrote an article in which he stated that—thanks to all kinds of technological developments—we should only have to work about 15 hours per week. But that doesn't happen. On the contrary, we still work long days and appear to be busier than ever. From his research, Graeber concludes that we think that a large part of our working hours are spent on useless tasks. According to participants in the study, some jobs have so little added value that he refers to them as bullshit jobs. He distinguishes five types of nonsense jobs:

1. **Waiters**: positions invented to make others (often the boss) appear more important, such as concierges, drivers, front desk employees, and operators. You can drive a car yourself, take a bus and pick up the phone.

2. **Bullies**: jobs that require a level of aggression, such as PR specialists, company lawyers and especially telemarketers. People from this last group are often uncomfortably aware that the purpose of their role is to sell useless prod ucts and services to other people.

3. **Fixers**: employees who must solve system errors, carelessness, and mistakes from others. An example of a fixer is someone who must copy texts by hand or make endless photo copies because there is no budget for a scanner.

4. **Box Checkers**: these jobs rightfully exist because they meet certain criteria, rules and regulations. One example is filling out forms

---

21 Graeber, David (2018). Bullshit jobs. Over zinloos werk, waarom het toeneemt en hoe we het kunnen bestrijden, Business Contact. Translated by Tracey Drost-Plegt.

> to prove that you ask people for their opinion and/or needs. Another is the work of (research) commissions that write reports about research results that then are shoved into a drawer. Box check jobs serve no other purpose than covering yourself and shifting responsibilities.
>
> 5. **Supervisors**, or the superfluous managers: supervisors manage a team that can work very well without being managed. Their role mostly leads to many extra forms, bureaucracy and unnecessary paperwork.

How does purpose work in real life?

It almost goes without saying that work should add value and be meaningful on one or all three levels of the purpose pyramid. However, in real life people often miss that. Research[22] performed in 2018 by Robert Dur and Max van Lent encompassing feedback from 100,000 employees across 47 countries shows, for instance, that eight out of every 100 employees believe their work makes no sense. Another 17 out of 100 doubt if their work has any use at all.

> **Annie:** *"I do have the feeling that it is a lot easier to experience meaning when you're a heart surgeon than when you're, for instance, an employee at a call center."*

People often think that purpose has to do with a specific profession; that some workplaces are more meaningful than others. However, research[23] shows that the content of the job, the industry, and the size of the organization have no influence on the feeling

---

22   Dur, Robert & Lent, Max van (2018). 'Socially Useless Jobs', Tinbergen Institute Discussion Paper, 18-034/VII. https://papers.ssrn.com/sol3/papers.cfm?abstract_id=3162569. Consulted on March 20, 2020.

23   Hansen, Morten (2018). Great at Work: How Top Performers Do Less, Work Better, and Achieve More, Simon & Schuster.

of purpose. In every industry and in every job there are people who experience their work as meaningful, while others in the same job or the same organization don't experience that same feeling. Take the example that we always use in our training course (add a link or a note here) about an employee at an emergency call center: Her most important job is to talk to people on vacation who are stranded, and to help them with their questions and problems. When she was asked what her best working experience had been, her reply was: "That was the day of the tsunami. With the entire team we talked to people, we comforted them, and we helped them with practical things. We were on the phone for 12 hours straight, without interruption. For me this experience made it very clear what I, as an employee at a call center, can mean for other people." The idea that certain industries and professions intrinsically have more purpose, is a myth.

Alignment

In short, purpose is about adding value as an organization, as a team, and as an employee; contributing to the bigger picture and wanting to make an impact. The better someone's personal purpose, the more closely aligned the purposes of both the team and the organization , the stronger everyone's feeling of meaning will be. The most relevant question is: for whom, and how, do we make a difference?

PILLAR 2: PEOPLE

People are social beings and need relationships with others. 'Friendship' and 'nice colleagues' are important reasons to work. This was reflected in the 2019 HBR article 'Does work make you happy?'[24]. Several worldwide studies show that unemployment affects our happiness. Besides a feeling of uselessness and the lack of a daily rhythm, people who don't work often experience a lack of social relationships. Feeling

---

24   https://hbr.org/2017/03/does-work-make-you-happy-evidence-from-the-world-happiness-report,

connected and working together with others in an environment where you feel safe and where you can be yourself is important for our happiness at work.

As far as we are concerned, the People pillar is about:
- Psychological safety
- Trust and attention

Psychological safety

In order to experience connection and happiness at work, psychological safety is a necessity. Psychological safety can best be described as the climate in which people treat each other respectfully, where employees feel at ease and where they feel confident to speak their mind without having to worry about possible reprisals. That doesn't mean that everybody must agree about everything, or that the atmosphere is always kind. Psychological safety is all about being able to express differences of opinions in a productive way and being able to handle conflict[25].

Trust and attention

Trust is based on the good in people. Like the owner of a construction company who told us during an interview: "When people are given trust, they belong. Sometimes I hear someone say that trust must be earned, but I think that's the wrong way around. If you start work somewhere, do you want to start with a dose of mistrust? Not me, that doesn't make me feel good about getting to work at all. It just starts with trust. And that's not hard at all. You can already start with it tomorrow." Giving sincere attention makes people feel that they are seen and valued.

---

25   Edmondson, Amy C. (2019). De onbevreesde organisatie, Business Contact. Translated by Albert Witteveen.

Pillar People

How to build more connection and trust? Discuss and answer the following questions:

- How connected are we as a team?
- To what extent do we have friends at work, and to what extent is that necessary?
- How safe do we feel?
- To what extent can we be ourselves?
- Do I belong?
- How much trust do we give to others, and how much do we receive from them?
- How do we personally contribute to an (un)safe work culture?
- How much time and attention do we have for one another?
- How much, and how often, do we give and receive appreciation?
- How much, and how often do we give and receive feedback?
- Do we treat people who make mistakes with encouragement or condemnation??
- How much room is there to learn?
- How do we set the right example our selves?

PILLAR 3: PROGRESS

Our results—or performance—also contribute to our happiness at work. When we see progress in our work we are more motivated and we feel more satisfaction. This is especially true when we make that progress in meaningful work, even in the smallest of steps[26]. However, we need to be able to influence

---

26   Amabile, Teresa & Kramer, Steven (2011). The Progress Principle: Using Small Wins to Ignite Joy, Engagement, and Creativity at Work, Harvard Business Review

and realize our performance for it to have a positive impact on our happiness at work. Among other things, progress is about:

- task related progression;
- personal growth and development;
- autonomy and ownership;
- flow.

Task-related progression

Task-related results are about getting your work done, checking off to-do lists, meeting a deadline, seeing results; achieving something. Everybody knows how good it feels to see the effects of your work, to have impact and feel a sense of satisfaction.

Personal growth and development

Progress is also about personal growth and development. Being challenged and learning new things contributes to a feeling of satisfaction. More than that, 'no room for development and learning' is a common reason why people look to change jobs. Most employees love challenges and want to be afforded the possibility to step out of their comfort zone into their growth or stretch zone. However, that step should not be too big, because then it can become a fear zone, and it is possible that it stops being a positive experience.

Autonomy and ownership

Achieving results leads to more happiness at work when employees feel involved and responsible for those results. That requires autonomy. Autonomy is the degree of independence and freedom that you receive to do your work in your own way, and at your own speed. It is one of the basic psychological needs[27][28], of a human being. Our own research

---

Press.

27   Ryan, Richard & Deci, Edward (2000). 'Self-Determination Theory and the Facilitation of Intrinsic Motivation, Social Development, and Well-Being', American Psychologist, 55 (1), pp. 68-78.

28   Broeck, Anja Van den, et al. (2016). 'A Review of Self-Determination Theory's

conducted in 2019 shows that autonomy is important in the Netherlands. The results show that self-employed people rate their happiness at work higher than people on a payroll. 83% of self-employed people experience autonomy, in contrast to 61% of those on a payroll[29]. This picture is not unique to the Netherlands. A publication of research from Researchnet[30] on autonomy in 27 countries shows that happiness at work grows with more autonomy. With more autonomy, the responsibility for—and involvement in—the end result also grows. So, autonomy paired with ownership yields the most happiness at work. The extent of autonomy that employees need for more happiness at work differs for every person, and can be dependent on the situation.

Flow

Under the 'progress' pillar, we also include the experience of flow. Research in the '70s and '80s by the American-Hungarian psychologist Mihaly Csikszentmihaly showed that the relationship between 'challenge' and 'ability' is closely linked to happiness at work. When a challenge and an employee's abilities are balanced in the right way, it creates a state of mind that Csikszentmihaly calls 'flow' (based on the metaphor of 'a stream that takes you with it'). In this mental state you are completely absorbed by what you do because you immediately see the successful results of your actions and activities.

> **Relationship Between Flow and Happiness at work**
>
> In our research, we also looked at the relationship between flow and happiness at work. As expected, we found that the relationship is positive. The more flow people experience in their

---

Basic Psychological Needs at Work', Journal of Management, 42 (5), pp. 1195-1229.

29   Veldhoen, Arie Pieter (2020). 'Hoe meet je werkgeluk?' from Handboek Werkgeluk, Ad Bergsma, Onno Hamburger & Edwin Klappe, Boom Uitgevers Amsterdam.

30   15. https://www.researchgate.net/publication/328890835_Self Employment_and_its_Relationship_to_Subjective_Well-Being (Consulted on Dec 1, 2021)

work, the more happiness they experience. Employees who seldom—or never—experience flow rate their happiness at work at an average of 6.1 on a scale from 1 – 10. Employees who experience flow very often/almost always, rate 8.1 on average. That's quite a difference. Sadly, this positive experience of flow at work is not true for the majority of workers. We found that only 43% of respondents experience flow in their work on a regular basis. That is a pity, because more flow not only provides more happiness at work, but it also turns out to be a good buffer against work-related stress—as long as the work pressure is not too high. In our research, respondents with high work pressure and 'high flow' in their work rated their happiness at work much higher on average than people who rated their pressure at work 'just right'.

How does progress work in real life?

According to research by Vertellis[31], 27% of 1035 employees surveyed in the Netherlands do not derive enough satisfaction from their work. 41% of the respondents say that they do not pay much attention to the progress they make on a daily basis, and one in three interviewees indicated that by Friday they cannot recall what they have done during the week. Bustle and stress are often the reason that people don't take the time to reflect on the tasks they did finish; therefore, they may achieve things but they don't experience the positive emotions or the feeling of happiness caused by their achievement.

---

31   Vertellis (n.d.). 'Kwart Nederlanders haalt te weinig voldoening uit zijn werk', Vertellis.nl. https://vertellis.nl/blogs/nieuws/kwart-nederlanders-haalt-te-weinig-voldoening-uit-zijn-werk. Consulted on April 10, 2020.

> **The 'Progress' Pillar**
>
> How do we experience progress? Discuss and answer the following questions
>
> - To what extent do we experience progress in meaningful work?
> - How do we make results visible?
> - How often do we consider our results and how do we celebrate them?
> - How do we make results and milestones of our learning process visible, and how do we celebrate them?
> - To what extent do we experience flow in our work?
> - What is needed to enable flow in our work?
> - To what extent do we experience autonomy, or the ability to decide for ourselves how we do our work?
> - How much responsibility do we assume?
> - How good are we at what we do?
> - To what extent do colleagues recognize each other's expertise?

PILLAR 4: POSITIVITY

Doing what you like, feeling energized, focusing on positivity and enjoying the here and now: that is the essence of the 'positivity' pillar. It is not just logical that this contributes to more happiness at work, there is also scientific proof for this. A positive outlook helps people both learn and cooperate more effectively, and it broadens their vision. In the long run, that makes them more agile and resilient. The opposite is also true: negative emotions cause people to turn more inward, to focus more on danger, and to close themselves to suggestions from other people or to working together[32].

There are a number of aspects under the 'positivity' pillar, such as:

- wellbeing and energy;
- focusing on positivity;
- getting enjoyment from the work that you do;
- having fun together.

Wellbeing and energy

Our physical fitness greatly influences our mental fitness, and vice versa. Even though we have not delved deeply into the different aspects of wellbeing, we want to point out that physical and mental fitness are also important for happiness at work. On one hand, well-being is about solving problems that are related to reducing the harm to people caused by stress, illness, accidents, and burnout. On the other hand, it is also about focusing on the prevention of these things before they cause harm. These include investing in a safe and healthy work environment, management of stress, stimulating a healthy lifestyle, and proactively ensuring a work environment in which happiness at work is normal. Happiness at work helps people to deal with the negative effects of stress.

> **The Influence of Thinking About Stress on Stress Itself**
>
> Body and mind have a strong influence on each other. How you feel about stress also determines how your body reacts to it. Research performed in America[33] that followed 30,000 adults for eight

---

32   Fredrickson, Barbara (2011). Positivity: Groundbreaking Research to Release Your Inner Optimist and Thrive, Oneworld Publications.
33   Loder, Vanessa (2015). 'Can Stress Kill You? Research Says Only If You Believe It Can', Forbes. https://www.forbes.com/sites/vanessaloder/2015/06/03/can-stress-kill-you-research-says-only-if-you-believe-it-can. Consulted on June 1, 2020.

> years found that it is not stress itself that increases the probability of death, but the way people feel about stress. When you think that stress is bad for you, your body reacts differently than if you think that it can help you. When you think positively about stress, the physical reaction of your body reacts the same way as when you are happy or brave— it produces a positive immune response, which promotes healing.

Focusing on positivity

Is the glass half full or half empty? How you look at this statement makes a big difference. From an evolutionary standpoint, people tend to focus more on negative things. We have to put more effort into positive thinking, but we can learn to do that—and it is worth the effort. Not just because a positive viewpoint makes us, and others, happier—positivity is contagious—but also because it contributes to success.

Deriving joy from the task at work

People who enjoy the work they do and the tasks that they perform experience more happiness at work. This comes from tasks that pique our curiosity, things that challenge us, and the possibility of experimenting and trying new things. It is no surprise that doing the work you enjoy contributes to your feelings of positivity in the moment, and so to your overall happiness at work.

Having fun together

Humor and having fun at work have a significant effect on positivity. Having fun motivates us and helps to put things in perspective. When you are already working hard and the pressure increases, a good joke is an excellent way to blow off some steam. It is a great alternative to complaining. Having fun together contributes to a positive working atmosphere. Cheerfulness and fun are contagious, and they ensure that you can handle challenges better. Doing something fun unexpectedly—surprising a colleague or sticking a funny poster next to the coffee machine—can do a lot for the morale of your team.

Contrary to popular belief, laughing and having fun are very effective ways to reach organizational and team goals. In spite of this knowledge, we often see in real life that organizations don't pay much attention to fun. It is not regarded as a way to reach targets. Often, when work pressure and stress in teams increases, laughter and having fun are deprioritized—even discouraged. In the end, that lack of a positive atmosphere affects the cooperation, performance, and the flourishing of the people striving to achieve their goals.

Those teams and organizations that make room for fun, even when things don't go well, are often more effective and have a better quality output. If you are a team that deals with innovation, there is another reason to keep having fun high on your agenda. The hormones that are released when we are enjoying ourselves influence the brain directly; they stimulate creativity and 'out of the box' thinking.

Pitfall of positivity

The 'positivity' pillar also has a pitfall; understanding that it is not about superficial fun. It is not the 'cool office' that makes people happy, or the good coffee, but creating a combination of atmosphere and work culture in which enjoyment and happiness at work take center stage. At most, the office space and the coffee are extensions of the underlying factors. When only these superficial elements are involved, such as a ping pong table, hanging up hammocks, or setting up a ball pit, you will quickly notice that these tactics don't work to create the outcomes of positivity that they aspire to. Even worse, they can have the opposite effect. In organizations where there is no safety or purpose, where no relevant results are achieved or celebrated, and where there is not much room for development, it's pointless to try remedying things by hanging up a hammock—and who on earth wants to have a crisis meeting in a ball pit? Some organizations have gone overboard in creating a special work environment and adding work benefits without addressing the underlying culture; like papering over the cracks. When you deploy happiness at work as a trick, then you truly miss the point. So, it is important to keep your eye on underlying reasons.

Fun at work at Tony's Chocolonely

Fortunately, there are a growing number of organizations that realize the importance of having fun and make it a conscious goal. One such example is Tony's Chocolonely. This company values fun at work and it is apparent in every aspect of the organization, from the lingo and the function titles that they developed together—such as Chief Chocolate Officer, Choco Evangelist and Choco-nocular—up to the decoration of the building, the processes, structures, and rituals. Everything they do happens with a wink, a joke, and a lot of fun. Tony's also experiences one of the negative side effects of happiness at work: sometimes people stay too long at a function because they love working there so much. They feel a connection with their colleagues, have fun, and pursue the mission of the organization—but when they are honest with themselves they are no longer experiencing challenges in the job itself, which is actually a necessity for them to perform at their best.

The 'Positivity' Pillar

Positivity is about the daily experience of enjoyment at work because people are more energetic and feel comfortable in their skin, and because they do work that makes them happy and/or by having fun with colleagues. Experiencing a positive work atmosphere can be identified in questions such as:

- To what extent is there room to laugh and to have fun?
- How often do we do (unexpectedly) fun things?
- How is the atmosphere in the teams, in the departments, in the organization?
- To which extent does the building

> contribute to wellbeing and having fun at work?
> - How do we maintain the energy level: what deflates people and what recharges them?
> - To which extent do we set a good example ourselves? Do we have fun at work and show it?
> - To which extent does making fun exceed the superficial?

Annie: "If I know who I work for, if I invest in co-operating with my colleagues, if I achieve more results and have fun more often, in the end that makes me happier at work. Is that correct?"

Happiness at work is about experiencing positive emotions about knowing that your work means something, being able to work well together with your colleagues, and achieving results. Without experiencing feelings of belonging your happiness at work will not increase. For example, suppose you were dreading a certain project or task, and despite your reservations you were able to successfully complete it. That can yield a lot of happiness at work, providing that you take a minute to consider and celebrate this milestone. Don't dive straight into the next project, because then you won't take the time to experience those positive feelings, the satisfaction that goes with the job well done. That also goes for collaboration with others. You must consciously experience the positive emotions that you feel from those collaborations. Reflecting, celebrating and acknowledging those feelings and experiences is what counts when it comes to happiness at work.

THE BIOLOGICAL SIDE OF THE FOUR PILLARS

Our feeling of happiness also has a biological side, namely our endocrine system. Hormones—or neurotransmitters—regulate all kinds of processes in our bodies. There are four neurotransmitters that have a direct link with the four pillars of happiness at work.

Serotonin and Purpose

Serotonin is the hormone that influences feelings of self-confidence, pride, and satisfaction. It aids good sleep and forms a buffer against fear and depression. Serotonin is released when you do things you are good at that you consider to be meaningful. Therefore, when making progress in meaningful work serotonin contributes to our feeling of significance.

Oxytocin and People

We refer to oxytocin as the love or attachment hormone. It is released during contact and interaction with other people, during intimacy and real connection. This hormone also makes us feel connected, trusting, and loyal.

Dopamine and Progress

Dopamine—also known as the rewarding or anticipation molecule—spurs us to action, just like the hormone adrenaline. However, dopamine also ensures that we enjoy the reaching of targets and deadlines. Our brains are constantly looking for forms of rewards without us realizing it. Dopamine is also related to autonomy because it makes us enjoy making decisions.

Endorphins and Positivity

Endorphins are our largest happiness messenger and an important natural painkiller. They also serve as an anti-stress hormone and are important for socialization, learning processes, and meaning. Endorphins are released with physical exercise, and when we laugh and have fun. It is clear, therefore, that there are biological links to explain why the four pillars contribute to happiness at work[34].

It's only by understanding the underlying biology of happiness, and reflecting upon the four pillars, that we can take steps towards building better, more positive work environments.

---

34   Graziano Breuning, Loretta (2015). Habits of a Happy Brain: Retrain Your Brain to Boost Your Serotonin, Dopamine, Oxytocin, & Endorphin Levels, Adams Media.

CHAPTER 4

A POSITIVE WORK CULTURE IS SOMETHING THAT YOU CREATE TOGETHER

If you want to increase happiness at work, then the four pillars of 'purpose', 'people', 'progress' and 'positivity' are the guidelines to changing behavior. This applies to individuals as well as to organizations. If you focus on creating the framework for change, you create a positive work culture that ensures that people and organizations can flourish, and eventually that will lead to better results. Building a positive work culture is not the responsibility of a single person, a specific function or department, the management or board of directors; this is something you work on together. However, the first step is to understand what a positive work culture is, how it is created and influenced, what your own role is and who is responsible for each aspect.

> **Culture is Like a Garden**
>
> A work, team, or organizational culture is about shared customs, ideas, and concepts. It is about how things go, or should go, and how these aspects of culture become visible in the language that is used and the behavior that is shown. Culture is directed by values and convictions, and is part of our everyday interactions where we instinctively copy, correct, and coach each other's behavior. An organizational culture is one which is shared by people, and it is always in a state of change. To consciously develop and change your culture in a specific direction is difficult, and takes a lot of time and effort. Think of your culture like a garden: whether you work in it or not, things will grow and bloom, this includes things you don't want. However, when you sow, weed, and cultivate purposely, something beautiful is created.

POSITIVE WORK CULTURE

The key to a successful and flourishing organization is a positive work culture. Therefore, it is imperative to build and maintain that culture in a structured way. What does that mean, exactly? We believe that in a positive work culture the employees come first, and the principles are clearly defined. The pillars of happiness at work (purpose, people, progress, and positivity) take central stage here. The organizational behavior and the behavior of the individual employees is focused on giving substance to and improving each of these pillars. This means that employees are aware of the purpose and the relevance of their work and put the communal interest first. They know why they do what they do and how they contribute to the bigger picture. That could be community-focussed goals, but the contribution to clear goals for teams, departments or organizations can also be meaningful. Employees connect with their colleagues; they pay attention to, and care about one another. They not only feel recognized and valued themselves, but they also recognize and value others. They are allowed to be themselves, they are allowed to be vulnerable, and they also accept and recognise the individuality and vulnerability of others. Each employee feels personally responsible, backed up by personal commitment, and they do everything within their power to achieve the goals of the organization, their colleagues and themselves. They experience the satisfaction of achieving results and personal development. Because of the positive work atmosphere—to which they actively contribute with a positive mindset—they have fun. Work provides them with more energy than they expend.

In short, a positive work culture is all about everybody's individual mindset and behavior being supported by the organization as a whole because:

- The principles, norms, values, and rules of conduct are clear and align with the pillars of happiness at work;

- The structures, processes, systems, and rituals of the organization support the desired behavior;

- Communication is open and transparent, and contributes to making the pillars a reality.

You can read more about culture and creating a positive work culture in chapters 11 and 12.

Difference between a positive culture and a strong one

People often confuse a positive organizational culture with a strong organizational culture. In a strong culture the principles are clear, just like in a positive culture. Employees know what the vision and mission are, and which values, norms, and rules of conduct apply. Everything fits together. In a strong culture the processes, structures, systems, communication, rituals, and day-to-day business also contribute to the realization of the stated principles. However, there is an important difference. In a strong culture the principles are not based on the pillars of happiness at work, while in a positive work culture it is all about giving substance to meaningfulness (purpose), connection (people), satisfaction (progress) and fun (positivity).

SHARED RESPONSIBILITY

Marian manages a facility team at a municipality. During our initial conversation she tells us that there is a lot of complaining in her department. "When a problem arises, they often come grumbling to me first, while they themselves know exactly how to solve it. Next to this, they also think that we don't do enough fun things together, but then if I organize something, half of them say they don't have time for it." With this information in the back of our mind, we ask Marian's team during the first workshop who, according to them, is responsible for happiness at work and a positive work culture. We use an imaginary line to divide the room in two and we ask the employees to choose a side: 'the organization's responsibility' on one side, or 'the responsibility of the individual employees' on the other. Some participants immediately choose a side, while others are in doubt and hang around in the center. In the end, the opinions are fairly divided and a good discussion follows about the responsibilities.

Organization has responsibility

Employees are part of a bigger picture; of a system with structures, processes, rituals, and habits that influence personal leadership and behavior. They also affect group dynamics and the behavior of others. In order to increase happiness at work and create a positive work culture, an organization as a system has a responsibility. That concerns offering psychological safety, openness, and transparency, giving space and autonomy, and creating a work environment in which people experience meaningfulness, challenge, satisfaction, connectedness, and fun.

Start with yourself

Culture arises from countless actions, interactions, and reactions, and gradually changes and develops from there. This means it is created jointly by leaders, managers, employees, and other people who interact with the organization at every level. Even though we cannot easily change the behavior of others, we can influence them by changing our own behavior. There is no change in culture without personal change. If you want to improve the situation at your work and you wish to increase happiness at work for yourself and your colleagues, you cannot lean back and pronounce that the organization must do something or say that you are responsible yourself and then do nothing. Working on a positive work culture means that you have to take action yourself and do things; change your behavior, be an example and inspire others.

> **Annie**: *"I think it's quite obvious that you are responsible for your own happiness at work. Why is it so important to ask people explicitly who is responsible?"*

By asking the question of who is responsible for happiness at work, we make people aware of the fact that they are primarily responsible and they must do something about it. The majority of people that are asked this question say that they are responsible themselves (in written, anonymous research that percentage is lower), but in real life they don't act on it. When we ask what actions people actually undertake in order to increase their own happiness at work, the question is often met with silence. Author and international speaker about happiness Leo Bormans says it beautifully: "It's not that we don't know what we must do. It's that we don't do what we know." And that's exactly what it's all about.

CHAPTER 5

OWNERSHIP OF YOUR HAPPINESS AT WORK

Taking responsibility starts with becoming aware of your own behavior. After that, it's about taking ownership and choosing the right mindset—then the real work begins. Taking responsibility also means you must change your behavior. There's a popular and applicable quote (apocryphally credited to Einstein) that the definition of insanity is doing the same thing over and over and expecting a different outcome. If you want to get to work on your own happiness at work, the four pillars—'purpose', 'people', 'progress' and 'positivity'—are your guidelines.

SELF-KNOWLEDGE AND THE QUADRANTS OF OWNERSHIP

Knowing yourself and having the skills to direct your own behavior form the foundation of personal leadership. We cannot always influence the situation that we are in, but we can influence how we feel about it and how we behave.

> **Chatter in Your Head**
>
> A lot of what we think is actually a story that we tell ourselves, a judgment or an opinion, and it is usually based on emotions, not on facts. The story we tell ourselves may not even be true. One of the participants in our workshop said that she recognizes this internal dialogue, and she finds that she tells herself both positive and negative stories on a regular basis. She said: "I'm practicing to regard this voice as something separate from myself. It is my ego that chatters all day long, praising me or tearing me apart. Usually, none of what it says is true. I named this ego 'Ruth'. Having given this voice a name, when she says things that are harmful or untrue, I can now tell the voice, 'Shut up, Ruth'. Somehow, it's easier to see her as separate from myself by giving her a name and I can see the stories more clearly for what they are: stories and not facts. I don't have to believe everything that Ruth says. So, actually I don't have to believe everything that I think." People who know themselves well are capable of looking at themselves from a distance and analyzing their own thoughts and emotions. 'Is it true what I'm thinking now, or are my emotions running away with me?' Self-awareness is a first step to more happiness at work.

It is necessary to take responsibility for your emotions, behavior, and happiness, but it is not always easy. Sometimes it works, sometimes it doesn't. The 'quadrants of ownership' model helps us to understand this[35]. This model was developed by Dan Diamond, and we have adjusted it for happiness at work. The model has two axes: an axis of influence or control (to which extent do you believe that you are in charge of what happens?) and an axis of meaning (to which extent do

---

35 Diamond, Dan (2015). Beyond Resilience: Trench-Tested Tools to Thrive Under Pressure, NogginStorm.

you do the things for yourself (I) or for something or someone else (we)?). These axes divide the model into four quadrants. Each of these quadrants represents a mental attitude. During the day we continuously shift between the mental attitudes that belong to the different quadrants. One moment we set ourselves up as the victim, the next moment we take the initiative to improve something, and we set ourselves up as a leader. This change in mindset happens so quickly we often don't even notice it happening. When you are aware of how you react in different situations, it can give you more control over your own attitudes and behaviors.

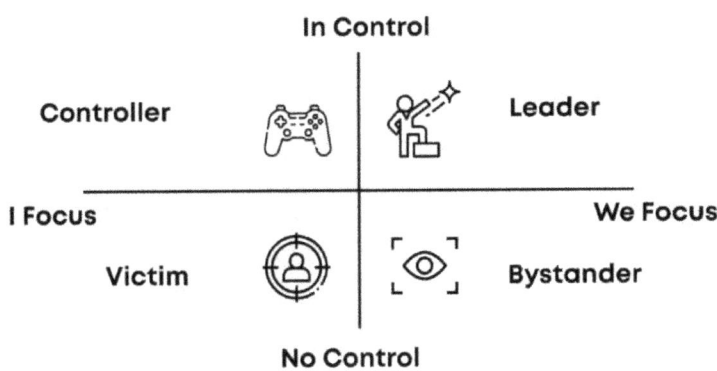

Quadrant 1: in control + I-focus = controller

If you are in the first (top-left) quadrant, you believe that you are in control, and that you are the most important person. You think and act only to benefit yourself, and you do not take other people or the greater good into account. You think that you have more rights than duties, you believe that you are better than other people, you don't like change, you see others as a threat, and you regard constructive criticism as a personal attack. You will say things like:

- "I am entitled to that!"/ "I deserve that."
- "That is not (or it is) part of my tasks, so I'm not going to do that (or, therefore you are not allowed to do that)."

- "I'm not interested in your criticism or feedback."
- "Here, it's everyone for themselves."
- "We have done it like that for years."
- "We already tried that; it's not going to work anyway."
- "If I don't take care of me, nobody will."
- "You got that promotion? I thought that I was going to get it."

Does the attitude of the controller lead to more happiness at work?

This attitude does not make you a favorite colleague of most people. You (subconsciously) assume scarcity, and you begrudge others their success, promotion, or fun. You are afraid to lose what you have now, and you hold on to it with all your might. With this attitude you do not contribute to the happiness of the team; you place your own interest and your own goals above those of others and the organization. In short, this attitude does not lead to good relationships at work, nor to good results for the team. Therefore, it is not a good strategy for more happiness at work.

Quadrant 2: no control + I-focus = victim

You find yourself in the victim quadrant when you think that you have no influence on what happens. You put yourself at the center, you reason from your own perspective, and you stay in your existing patterns. You do things for yourself in order to protect your own interests, and you are reactive. Fear is often your biggest motivation. With this attitude you let your success depend on others. You say things like:

- "The manager is responsible for the atmosphere in the team."
- "The organization must make sure that I have less work pressure."
- "My boss is responsible for whether I feel good at work."
- "Whatever I do, it is never good enough."

- "Of course, that happens to me, I always have bad luck."
- "Somebody else must solve this problem."
- "Promotion? Hah, those nice things never happen to me."

Does the victim mindset lead to more happiness at work?

Sometimes it really feels good to dwell in the role of victim. And it's not too bad if this attitude doesn't last long, but if you get stuck in there it will have a negative effect on your self-confidence. You start believing more and more that you need others. Consider how unpleasant this reactive attitude can be for your colleagues. In the end it does not contribute to your happiness at work, nor to that of your colleagues.

Quadrant 3: no control + we-focus = bystander

As a bystander you think that you have no control, but you are geared towards 'we'; focussed on the greater interest. You have the best of intentions, but you do not believe that you can change anything, that you can make a difference. You're not actively involved, but passively. You can hear yourself say things such as:

- "I would like to, but I'm not in a position to do so."
- "How can this be, someone (management, the board of directors, the government) should do something about this."
- "I do the best I can but, well... that problem really is nothing I can fix..."
- "I wish I could do something about it, but it's not up to me."
- "I did what we had agreed upon, so I'll wait and see until I get the next assignment. I'll be happy to do that then. In the meantime, I'll play solitaire."
- "Nice that you have a promotion, I don't think I'll ever be able to get one."

Does the attitude of the bystander lead to more happiness at work?

If you find yourself with this attitude at work, then you've actually already quietly quit. You show up at work every day, but when it comes to taking that extra step and taking the initiative, you don't bother because you feel that you have no influence anyway. Such a feeling of powerlessness does not lead to decisiveness, and it also does not contribute to a feeling of progress and satisfaction.

Quadrant 4: in control + we-focus = leader

In the leader mindset you want to make a difference and therefore you take the initiative to make things better. You don't care about who gets credit for it. In fact, you enjoy it when others are successful. You take responsibility for yourself and for others. This quadrant is not about effacing yourself or always putting other people's interests over those of your own. This quadrant includes taking responsibility for your own health, wellbeing, and boundaries. In the long run, taking care of yourself is good for everyone else as well. If you choose this attitude, you say:

- "Okay, this situation is not ideal. What can I do to help?"
- "This went wrong. What's my part in this and what can I improve on it?"
- "My own growth and development are my responsibility, so I have a proposal that will also be better for the team."
- "My colleagues will be stuck if I don't finish this, so I'll stay for another hour today."
- "I'm going home on time today so I can recharge."
- "I see that you're having a hard time with this, how can I help you?"
- "Congratulations on your promotion, you did very well!"

Does the attitude of the leader contribute to more happiness at work?

The attitudes and behaviors in this quadrant give you the most happiness at work. In this mental attitude we experience meaning, connection, and satisfaction. You feel involved with the organization and its goals, and you are prepared to step it up if necessary. You also work well with others because you are more involved with your colleagues and their wellbeing. Most probably your colleagues like you too. That is because you are prepared to help, and you have the best interest at heart for the team and the organization. This is a twofold advantage: this attitude makes you happy and is to the advantage of the organization.

> **Exercise: Getting a Grip on Your Attitude**
>
> You can practice getting more of a grip on your own attitude, but how do you go about doing that? Start by listening to your own internal dialogue for one or two weeks. What are you telling yourself? Over this time, we also recommend that you observe your own behavior. Ask yourself the following questions:
> - If I hear myself saying this or observe myself doing that, in which quadrant does that fit?
> - How does that feel?
> - Is this the quadrant that I want to be in? If not, in which quadrant do I want to be?
> - What is the behavior that goes with that?
> - What can I do differently?
> - What would be a great solution or outcome right now?[end text box]

THE EFFECT OF THE GOOD EXAMPLE

If you would like to contribute to a positive work culture, then participating in complaining at the coffee machine does not help. Trying to stop the grumbling does help. People won't always be grateful for that, and you can be perceived as a goody-goody. Still, it is worth the effort because it takes only a single person following your good example to have a huge impact. As you go through your work life, try to find people who are likeminded. Who among your colleagues wants to stop complaining? Do it together! Help each other in maintaining the desired behavior of not complaining. What else can you come up with to facilitate this new desired behavior for others? To stay with the example of not complaining: you could post a sign at the coffee machine that reads: 'Complaint-free zone. We don't complain here but we do laugh! Oops, you complained by accident? Then throw a dollar in the jar. If it's full, we buy muffins.'

Leading by example is always effective. Sharon, a participant in one of our workshops, tells us: "I do understand that you say that the model is intended for your own consciousness and that you're not supposed to use it for others. I would find it irritating if a colleague told me: 'Don't play the victim.' Even if it was true at that moment, I would prefer to come up with that myself, one way or another. However, I do like the model a lot so I was wondering how I could explain it to my colleagues without being a know-it-all. I started thinking about it and what I came up with in the end is that I simply drew the model on the whiteboard in my office. Several colleagues have already asked what it means and how it works. They now apply it too. It is really neat to see how such a thing then spreads. And quite honestly, we sometimes forget about it too. Then we fall back into that role of a victim or in one of the other quadrants. But all we have to do is remind each other by saying 'quadrant'. Very handy, colleagues."

CHAPTER 6
DEVELOP YOUR GROWTH MINDSET

Math teacher and researcher Marloes van Hoeve from the Netherlands has switched jobs radically a few times during her career. She graduated as a geologist, worked as a civil servant, and then jumped tracks to education. She received a degree in geology and later in mathematics. Still, she was always afraid that she would be judged as being 'not professional enough': "The fear of failure was like a common thread running through my life. Until I discovered that this fear had everything to do with my fixed mindset and that there was an alternative for it that was a lot more interesting. That changed my world and that didn't only make me a better teacher, it also made me a lot happier at work and in the rest of my life."

WHAT IS MINDSET?
Your mindset is your point of view, your opinions, convictions, or way of thinking about how reality is constructed. It is the way in which you look at the world and yourself. Mindset is often based on deeply-rooted basic convictions that are so self-evident for you that you are not even aware of them. In fact, often you don't even know that other convictions and perspectives are possible.

Fixed and growth mindset

As a young researcher, professor in psychology Carol Dweck investigated how people deal with mistakes[36]. She assumed that nobody enjoys failure and that therefore everybody has their own strategy to avoid mistakes. She was especially curious about the different strategies that people use to prevent failure, or how to deal with it when it does happen. However, she discovered by accident that a number of her test subjects were not averse at all to failure. On the contrary, they seemed to embrace making mistakes. When she started researching what caused this unexpected response, she discovered a difference in mindset.

Fixed mindset

Fixed mindset is the conviction that your qualities, intelligence, personality, and character are set in stone. With a fixed mindset you feel that 'this is it' for the rest of your life when it comes to talents and the capacities that were given to you. You continuously have the feeling that you have to prove yourself. With a fixed mindset you also have the feeling that you cannot fix a mistake, and that if you have to make an effort to get something done this means that you are not good enough.

Growth mindset

The opposite of a fixed mindset is what Dweck refers to as a growth mindset. With a growth mindset you believe that you can develop your basic qualities by pushing yourself and learning new things. You don't view your mistakes as failures, but rather as a way to improve.

Recognizing the two mindsets

In her book, Dweck creates the impression that a fixed or a growth mindset strongly determines how you lead your life in general. We see this through a slightly more nuanced lens. Mindset is never a label, but it always is a snapshot. It differs in time, per state of mind, and per subject—and you can change

---

36 Dweck, Carol (2015). 'Carol Dweck Revisits the "Growth Mindset"', Edweek. org. https://www.edweek.org/ew/articles/2015/09/23/carol-dweck-revisits-the-growth-mindset.html. Consulted on January 22, 2020.

your mindset over time and develop a more growth-oriented mindset. In the following diagram[37] you will find an overview of the way in which you react to things like skills, challenges, behavior, collaboration, feedback, and setbacks, based on the different mindsets and what their effect is.

Fixed Mindset	Thinking About	Growth Mindset
You're born with skills, they are fixed.	Skills	You develop skills with hard work, you can always improve.
Challenges must be avoided. They show that there is something you cannot do.	Challenges	Challenges must be embraced. They are an opportunity for growth.
Not necessary; you do that only if you're not good enough (as a result you give up quickly)	Making an effort, pushing yourself	Essential; the path to improvement (as a result you learn to persevere)

---

37 Hoeve, Marloes van (2019). 'Mindsets en wiskunde', Euclides 94 (4). https://nvvw.nl/euclides/jaargang_94/#Euclides944. Consulted on 22 January 2020.

	Reacting On	
Defensive, taking things personally.	Feedback	Useful, you can learn from it.
Blame others, becoming discouraged.	Setbacks	Setbacks are learning possibilities, a wake-up call to work harder next time.
	Effect On	
Status quo remains.	Thinking	Stimulates growth.
Avoiding challenges.	Behavior	Learning from mistakes, like to take on challenges.
Fear of failure.	Opinions	Everything can always be better.
I must show what I can do and what I can do better.	Collaboration	Nice, that I can learn from them.

MISUNDERSTANDINGS AND PITFALLS

The popularity of thinking in fixed and growth mindset—and Dweck's work—has increased over the past few years, which is great. With the increase of that popularity, we also see that a growth mindset has come to be regarded as desirable and a fixed mindset as undesirable. That leads to a number of pitfalls.

Misunderstanding 1: A fixed mindset is undesirable

With the idea that a growth mindset is better, it appears as though we should always strive for that and always avoid a fixed mindset. But we shortchange ourselves with that idea; a fixed mindset is also part of human nature, and it is not necessary to always have a growth mindset about everything. Actually, a growth mindset is especially relevant for the areas in which we want to grow and want to develop ourselves.

Misunderstanding 2: A growth mindset is a goal in itself

A growth mindset helps you to learn new things and to change, because with this mindset we experience the learning process and all that comes with it as useful and positive. However, when a growth mindset is perceived as 'better' and desirable, people will then pretend or mimic that mindset, which is not conducive for the learning process.

Misunderstanding 3: Feedback based on growth mindset is only about putting in the effort

A growth mindset is stimulated when you compliment people for the effort that they put into something. However, focusing solely on progress without mentioning results can lead to the idea that 'putting in effort' is enough, while the result is important too. One example of this is Microsoft's work on growth mindset, where they focussed on taking 'smart risks'. This means they were not rewarding risky behavior, but were encouraging people to take risks which had the potential to have positive outcomes for the business.

Misunderstanding 4: Using a fixed mindset as an excuse

It can also happen that someone is wrongly labeled as having a 'fixed mindset', for instance when a manager thinks that an employee takes too long to learn something. You can imagine that the learning process of the employee is compromised when they are labeled with a fixed mindset.

> "WHETHER YOU THINK YOU CAN, OR YOU CAN'T — YOU ARE RIGHT."
>
> – HENRY FORD –

HOW DO YOU DEVELOP A GROWTH MINDSET?

A growth mindset is a basis for learning new things and changing behavior. Four things that help to develop a growth mindset are:

1. self-knowledge;
2. knowledge of how the brain works: neuroplasticity;
3. celebrating mistakes;
4. giving and receiving the right kind of feedback.

Self-knowledge

Self-knowledge is relevant here too. Everybody has set convictions and it is important to know, for instance, to which extent you think that your intelligence and personality are changeable. Therefore, it is handy to understand when you approach things with a fixed mindset and when you approach them with a growth mindset. Do you feel fear when facing a new challenge, or does it give you energy? Are you looking for excuses when there is something you cannot do right away, or do you see them as possibilities to learn something? Do you regard feedback as criticism or as a way to learn? How do you deal with someone who is better than you are?

Test your mindset

If you would like to get a better insight into your own mindset, the following test may help. When you fill this out, you need to realize that the result is a snapshot, not a label. This means that under different circumstances your results can be quite different. For that reason, we encourage you to take the test again at a later stage.

Agree or disagree?

1. I have the power to expand or improve my skills and talents
   (agree: 2 points, disagree: 1 point)

2. I like it when I can do something effortlessly
   (agree: 1 point, disagree: 2 points)

3. I love to learn things, even when that means I make mistakes
   (agree: 2 points, disagree: 1 point)

4. I feel less discouraged than others if I must put more effort into something
   (agree: 1 point, disagree: 2 points)

5. I can learn new things, but that doesn't change how smart I am
   (agree: 1 point, disagree: 2 points)

6. I love it when I have to think hard about something and really put effort into learning
   (agree: 2 points, disagree: 1 point)

7. When I think something is difficult, I like to spend more time on it
   (agree: 2 points, disagree: 1 point)

8. I enjoy doing something that I can do perfectly
(agree: 1 point, disagree: 2 points)

Result

8-12 points: you have a tendency towards a fixed mindset regarding growth and development.

12-16 points: you have a tendency towards a growth mindset regarding growth and development.

Exercise: Getting to Know Your Growth Mindset

Take a certain period, for example a week, to check how you react in certain situations. Don't just take the easy examples, but also look at the difficult moments. To which scenarios do you think it's easy to react from a growth mindset, and when do you have a fixed mindset? If you write it down in a journal this will give you more insight. What are the possible reactions in certain situations, both from a fixed and a growth mindset? Try them both and see the effect.

Tip

In order to learn the difference, you can stick the two mindsets with their differences on your mirror. This way you are reminded every morning about how you can react.

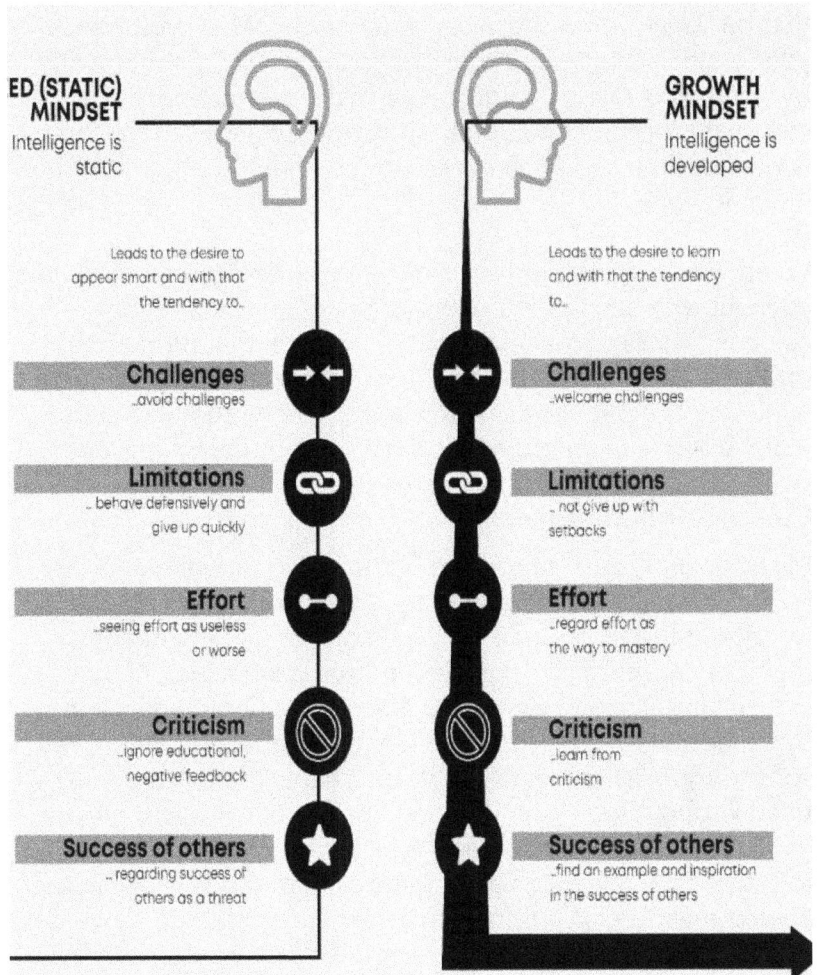

Neuroplasticity: how our brains work

It has been proven that our brains are not 'fixed'. It turns out that our capacities, intelligence, and skills can change over the course of our entire lifetime. Neurological research shows that our brain works the same as a muscle. When you train your brain, it becomes larger and stronger. The phenomenon by which your brain can grow and make new connections is called neuroplasticity. Even though neuroplasticity in children is greater than in adults, everybody can learn during his or her entire lifetime.

When we do something for the first time, synapses in our brain connect with each other. A new connection is made that you can imagine as a small path. When you use that path more often, try out and practice that new behavior, this becomes a habit and the path becomes 'bigger'. The more new things that we learn, the more new connections our brain makes.

Celebrating mistakes

Mistakes and failures promote our learning process, and that makes them useful. Instead of trying to cover them up—which we often tend to do—we would be better off celebrating them, because it makes us even better at what we do. Van Hoeve also started celebrating mistakes in her lessons, and that made her work a lot more fun: "I used to prepare my lessons to the smallest details, I did not allow myself to do anything wrong. Ever since I learned about the fixed and growth mindset, I let go of that idea. I try to solve math problems together with my pupils and I'm not afraid of not knowing the answer anymore. All mistakes that are being made, I leave on the blackboard, including my own. That's how they learn how valuable they are. Together we analyze them, and we come up with new strategies to deal with them. This way it doesn't only help me but also my students. Their learning effect has increased a lot because of this."

> **Making mistakes and reflections**
>
> To truly learn from your mistakes, it is important to take a minute and reflect on them. Questions you could ask are:
> - How do I deal with mistakes?
> - How do I feel when I make a mistake?
> - When did I make my last mistake?
> - To what extent does the chance of making a mistake stop me from learning new things?
> - How do I deal with mistakes from people in my team?
> - What do I find challenging?
> - When did I think of a fixed mindset as being safe or pleasant?

The importance of feedback

The way you give feedback to yourself and to others influences your mindset, and that of others. When you emphasize the naming of someone's characteristics, that then leads to a fixed mindset. It doesn't matter whether this feedback is negative or positive. Even compliments such as 'you are so smart/bright/funny' lead to a more fixed mindset. That is because you have assigned characteristics to a person as if they are set, and that leads to giving a person the feeling—consciously or subconsciously—that they always must meet certain expectations. However, when you focus on the process, that appeals to a growth mindset. Expressions such as 'you do this well', 'you can still learn this' and 'you say that in a funny way' allow for more space.

Therefore, if you want to stimulate yourself and others for growth, feedback about the process works better. In this overview[38] you can see the difference:

Fixed Feedback	Growth Feedback
'You are so smart'	'You did that well'
'I'm so stupid'	'What did I miss?'
'I really cannot do this'	'I must try this more often'
'You really are a lot better at this than I am'	'You have interesting ideas for improvement'
'He/she is better than I am'	'What can I learn from him/her?'
'Not everybody can do everything, just do the best you can'	'By just trying things, you learn how to do it'
'I/you cannot do it'	'I/you cannot do it yet'

> **Practicing Feedback**
>
> If you want to give yourself and others better feedback, first take some time to observe and consider what you say, and what sort of feedback you receive from others. Do this without judgment, using the questions:
> - Is this feedback directed to characteristics or to the process?
> - What effect does it have? What do I see?
> - Which feedback do I find easier?
> - What can I change and what would be the effect of that?

---

38   Hoeve, Marloes van (2019). 'Mindsets en wiskunde', Euclides 94 (4). https://nvvw.nl/euclides/jaargang_94/#Euclides944. Consulted on 22 January 2020.

Effect of growth mindset on happiness at work

A growth mindset leads to more happiness at work because it makes changing and learning easier. You have a more positive attitude towards making mistakes and you enjoy the learning process more. You regard yourself and others more realistically, and with more tolerance. A growth mindset also facilitates collaboration. You can deal better with feedback, learn more from each other, and you do not experience competition. That leads to greater connection and psychological safety, and has a positive effect on experiencing progress. When you work together on growth mindset as a group, it also makes you more aware of the successes that you achieve together—which ultimately provides more satisfaction.

CHAPTER 7

HOW YOU CAN CHANGE YOUR BEHAVIOR PERMANENTLY

"After your workshop about happiness at work I intended to give positive feedback more often," account manager Sally, one of our participants, told us. "But in all honesty, I didn't keep it up for even three weeks. Maybe two weeks. The minute the account plans had to be made and I was swamped, I just forgot about it." A relatable story. We have all had good intentions that started with enthusiasm, but in the end, those good intentions fizzled out.

DESIGNING BEHAVIOR MAKES CHANGE EASY

If you want to have a different outcome—for instance if you want to have more happiness at work than you experience now—you have to change your behavior. We often think that it's difficult to change. If we look at our New Year's resolutions, it seems that changing our behavior is difficult. Only 8% of people are successful in maintaining the new behavior for extended periods of time. This means the other 92% do not succeed. There are many reasons why our good intentions go up in smoke: We simply forget what it was that we wanted to do differently, we change our minds because we received new information, or we no longer find the idea attractive once we put it into practice. Still, changing your behavior is not as difficult as we believe it to be. It can be done, as long as we know how to do it and if we design the change well. If you set out your steps clearly and start with a growth mindset, you significantly increase your chance of success.

Behavior has three boosters: motivation, ability, and environment[39][40]. Each of these factors are needed simultaneously in order to initiate a behavior[41]. Motivation is about wants: ask yourself why you want to change your behavior, and what will the new behavior bring you? Ability is about whether you are capable or able to show the behavior. Environment relates to the circumstances that evoke the behavior. These are sometimes referred to as 'triggers'.

> **IF YOU ALWAYS DO WHAT YOU ALWAYS DID, YOU WILL ALWAYS GET WHAT YOU ALWAYS GOT.**

MOTIVATION

Motivation is what makes people take action in the first place. It is the inner urge to reach a certain goal. Motivation is capricious and can fluctuate a lot during the day; many people are more motivated to tackle difficult jobs in the morning than at the end of the workday. Keeping your goal clear and concrete helps maintain your motivation.

---

39 Poiesz, Theo (1999). Gedragsmanagement. Waarom mensen zich (niet) gedragen, Inmerc Uitgeverij.
40 Tiggelaar, Ben (2018). De Ladder, Tyler Roland Press.
41 Fogg, B.J. (2020). Tiny Habits, the small changes that change everything

> **Helpful Questions to Clarify Your Goal**
>
> - What do I want to change?
> - Why do I want this?
> - Is this goal really important for me?
> - How is reaching this goal going to improve my life?
> - How is reaching this goal going to give me a good feeling?
> - What does the desired outcome look like, and how will it differ from where I am now??

The difference between a goal and behavior

Setting goals does not automatically lead to behavioral change. Research shows that people abandon their goals because the behavior that is necessary to reach the goal is not outlined clearly enough. For a better chance at success you need to translate your goal into concrete behavior. Suppose that your goal is to increase happiness at work through better collaboration. That appeals to you because you think that it will make your work more enjoyable, and that it will make you more effective and productive. You then need to ask, "What behavior is needed to reach my goal?" By outlining the behavior concretely, it becomes clear exactly what steps you need to take to achieve your goal. Outlining each step in turn increases the chance that you will successfully achieve your goals. In this example you might write down three actions you want to take to improve your happiness at work:

1. Choose to give positive feedback at least once a week to a colleague
2. On Monday, share what you are working on
3. Ask a colleague every day at the coffee machine how they are feeling

How do we check that our goals have clearly defined, concrete behaviors? Ask yourself the following:

1. Can I make a video of it?
2. Can I do it here and now?

For example, if your goal is happiness at work through better collaboration, can you do that here and now? Or can you make a video of yourself 'better collaborating'? You cannot. This is a goal, not a behavior. It is not concrete enough to trigger a behavior. Reformulate your goal to ensure the answers to those questions are 'yes'.

Another example: "My goal is to increase happiness at work by giving more positive feedback." You can make a video of yourself giving positive feedback, and you can do it here and now. This is a concrete behavior towards creating more happiness at work.

Every Behavior Results in a Reward

Every behavior has a reward, otherwise we wouldn't do it. However, it is not always clear what that reward is. If you want to show or stop a certain behavior, it is helpful to discover what the associated reward is. People do things that bring no long-term reward to them at all. For example: criticizing a colleague in a nasty way may give you a sense of superiority in the short term, but it doesn't lead to more connection and happiness at work in the long term. That brief positive emotion—caused by a feeling of superiority—is the reward. When we are rewarded, this causes us to repeat this behavior more often, in spite of the fact that the behavior does not lead to happiness at work. However, if the reward is strong enough, we will repeat the behavior over and over again.

Increasing motivation

You can increase your motivation by:

- having a clear view of what your goal is and what benefits it will bring you;
- keeping track of your progress by writing it down;
- telling others what you want to start doing;
- performing the new behavior together with other people, in this way you can help and motivate each other;
- linking a reward to the new behavior.

> **Annie:** "So, I can arrange that reward for myself too?"

Of course you can! If you want to build a 'new behavior' into something you do regularly, it helps if you think about the reward in advance. How will the new behavior make you feel good? For example: your new desired behavior is to give a compliment to a colleague every day. After you have completed the new behavior, take a moment to feel proud of having achieved it. This can be anything from saying, "You did a great job, well done," or a simple "Woohoo!" Linking a reward that makes you feel good to a new—and desired—behavior, and acknowledging that positive feeling will help you repeat the new behavior the next day as well.

ABILITY

The second factor that is needed for behavior is ability, also referred to as capacity or skill. What we mean here is: are you able to achieve the desired behavior? Is it within your physical or cognitive abilities? Say you would like to have lunch with your colleague more often. You both need to be available during lunch time, there must be a location where you can have lunch together, and you both must have something to eat. All these factors combined makes it possible to have lunch together.

If you lack the capacity to show the desired behavior then you will not make progress on your particular goal. Not having capacity can manifest as:

- insufficient time;
- insufficient financial means;
- not being able to do it physically;
- the fact that the skill demands more creative or mental energy;
- the fact that the skill requires adjustment of your existing routines.

If you are not successful in starting or maintaining a new behavior, consider whether it is caused by one of these five reasons. This might help you to identify what needs to change in order for you to create the desired behavior.

Increasing ability

To increase your ability you can learn to get better at practicing your desired behavior. What do you need to be able to do to begin a new behavior? How can you best learn and practice that? For example, if you want to give more positive feedback but you are not confident in how to do that, you can take a course on the subject and practice what you learned in real life. Learning increases your ability. Another way to increase your ability is to make the behavior smaller or more fun, thus making it easier. Start with something you already know and enjoy. Following on from the previous example, you could start by complimenting a colleague every day. This repeated action, achieved regularly will build your confidence and will support you to keep going. By breaking down the behavior and making it smaller it is easier to integrate it into something you do regularly. After you have completed the smaller steps, you may soon notice that it takes less effort. This helps your drive towards the new behavior and shows it is time to take the next (small) step. For example, once you have successfully complimented your colleagues—and it becomes a regular occurence—you can then try giving positive feedback to people you don't know as well.

> **Helpful Questions to Increase Your Ability**
>
> - Is my desired behavior easy?
> - Do I enjoy doing it?
> - Can I already do it, or do I still have something to learn?
> - Am I taking achievable steps?
> - How can I make those steps even smaller?
> - What might stop me from being able to achieve the new behavior? What obstacles may I run into? How can I prepare for, or overcome, those?
> - What can I learn? From whom or how will I learn in order to get better at this?

ENVIRONMENT

The third booster of behavior is your environment. This is about things around you that elicit (desired) behavior, also known as triggers. Our environment influences our behavior a lot more than we think; many of our habits are based on it. Think about everything you do when you go to work in the office; you put down your bag, turn on your computer, get a cup of coffee. When you work from home, the trigger that turns on your 'normal' behavior—in this case the fact that you arrive at the office—is not present, thus your behavior will be different. You can use this if you want to change your behavior and ingrain a new behavior. Let's take a simple example: suppose that you would like to drink water more often instead of coffee. Something in your environment needs to change to remind you of that. You could stick a post-it on your coffee mug with 'water' written on it. If you then get water instead of coffee often enough, this will turn into an automatic behavior when repeated often enough.

Another practical way to use the environment and the triggers is by linking your new desired behavior to an existing habit. You formulate your new behavior as follows: 'If I do this… (existing habitual behavior), then I will also do… (new, desired behavior). To stay with the example: 'If I get a cup of coffee at the office, I will also drink a glass of water.' Getting the coffee is a behavior that is already triggered by coming into the office, and adding a glass of water is only one small extra step.

If you want to do things differently, triggers in your environment are incredibly important. Usually those are the ones we forget to prepare and utilize when trying to change our behavior. We want something and we are able to do it, but we forget about our desired change because we have not adjusted our environment. The more triggers we build into our environment that elicit the behavior, the better. Therefore, we need to think deeply about our environment and 'design' that new behavior, including the triggers.

> **Helpful Questions for Good Triggers**
>
> - How do I remind myself to change/add the new behavior?
> - Which things in my environment can I change so that I will be reminded of the behavior?
> - Where can I write down that I was successful?
> - Are there things in my environment that will prevent my desired behavior?
> - What is the existing behavior to which I can link my new behavior (when I do this, then I will also do…)?
> - How am I going to give myself a positive feeling if I was successful?

MAKING UP FOR A SHORTAGE

If you are good at something (ability is high), then you are probably motivated to get even better at it. Behavior has an influence on ability: if you do something more often, you get better at it. Because the factors are linked and they influence each other, an increase in one can sometimes make up for a shortfall in the other. The triggers we spoke about should be present in all cases. An example: If you are very motivated to discover how you can use your beautiful new laptop but are not very good at it because you haven't worked with this new model, your ability is low but your motivation is high.

Chances are you're going to do it anyway because you really want to. The reverse is possible too: if you want to do something that you are not really motivated to do, then that lack of motivation can be balanced by 'high ability'; a behavior that comes easily for you. Another example: making a payment is not something that people enjoy. Receiving a request for payment via an app (the trigger) makes it so easy that most people make the payment right away.

EFFECTIVELY DESIGNING A CHANGE IN BEHAVIOR

To change behavior it is important that you carefully design your new desired behavior. Careful design gives you the greatest chance for success. Let's list the design steps:

- **Step 1**: investigate your motivation. What is your specific goal? Why would you like to have this outcome? What behavior is needed for achieving that goal?

- **Step 2**: investigate your ability. Can you perform the behavior? Do you have the necessary skills? Or do you need things to make it easier and smaller?

- **Step 3**: search for the right triggers in the environment. What in the environment is going to ensure that you do not forget the intended behavior? What is going to elicit your new behavior?

Annie: *"Can I use this method to help other people change their behavior? I have a few ideas for some colleagues…"*

You're not alone in wanting to change someone else's behavior. However, behavioral scientists say that you should focus on your own behavior. You have more influence on your own behavior, and your behavior has an effect on others too: it pays to set a good example.

CHAPTER 8
BEHAVIOR AND HAPPINESS AT WORK: FOCUS ON THE PILLARS

Once you are aware of and are taking responsibility for your own mindset and behavior, you can start working on your happiness and start doing things that make you truly happy, based on the four pillars: 'purpose', 'people', 'progress' and 'positivity'.

> **🏋 Excercise: The Circle of Happiness at Work**
> In order to understand what you can do to increase your happiness at work, you must first know your current situation. This exercise will help by giving you insight into the most significant contributors to your happiness at work, thus where you can improve the most[42].

---

42 This exercise is based in the happiness at work pyramid as described in: Hamburger, Onno & Bergsma, Ad (2011). Gelukkig Werken, Uitgeverij Boom/Nelissen.

Purpose, People, Progress, Positivity.

Step 1: Copy the Circle of Happiness at Work onto a piece of paper. Rate each of the four pillars from lowest to highest on a scale of 1 to 10. Don't think about this too long. Now that you have rated each pillar you can dive into what this score means for you.

Step 2: Answer the following questions and write the answers next to your Circle:

- What do the different pillars mean for you?
- Which pillar did you score high, and which did you score low?
- What are your reasons for your high score? The low score?
- Where do you see the most room for improvement?
- For which pillars are you already actively doing something?
- On which of the pillars are you already showing a growth mindset?
- How would you score your happiness at work as a whole?
- Look back at the score for each pillar. How can you use those to improve your overall happiness at work score?
- What is/are the behavior/s you need to begin? Is that behavior easy, can you define even smaller steps?
- What triggers in your environment can you introduce in order to remind yourself of the desired behavior?

> FOCUS ON EACH OF THE PILLARS:
>
> HOW DO YOU FEEL ABOUT EACH OF THEM?
>
> WHICH OF THE PILLARS YIELDS THE MOST IF YOU DO SOMETHING ABOUT IT?
>
> WHAT IS THE RELATED BEHAVIOR?

IMPROVING ON – PURPOSE

Remember the story of the cleaner at NASA in the 1960s? When asked what his job was, he answered, "I'm helping to put a man on the moon." On July 20, 1969, he was successful. His feeling of purpose far exceeded his actual work. He was able to connect the work he was doing to the larger purpose of his organization. What can you do to increase your sense of purpose?

You can do the following:

- Act based on your values;
- Connect your personal purpose to your work;
- Understand what your purpose means to you and how you can make it practical.

Act based on your values

To experience purpose it is important to stay true to yourself, to what is important for you. Your personal values serve as a compass for what you consider to be good and worthwhile. Is it about making the world a better place? Or about making money to support your family? This is personal, and there is no 'correct' answer.

> **Exercise: What Are Your Values?**
>
> Finding your values can be like a treasure hunt. The values are out there, somewhere. You just have to discover them. The map to your treasure could contain the following questions:
>
> 1. Think about a special moment in your life, a moment when you were very proud or happy. What happened, exactly? What did you value about that experience? What was present in that moment?
> 2. Now reverse it: think about a time when you were very angry or upset, a moment of deep unhappiness. What were you missing at that moment? Which values were not present then[43]?
> 3. Search for a list of values on the internet. There are

---

43   This method has been copied and adjusted from: Jeffrey, Scott (n.d.). '7 Steps to Discover Your Personal Core Values', ScottJeffrey.com. https://scottjeffrey.com/personal-core-values. Consulted on May 9, 2020.

> many lists to help you in the right direction. Which are the words that appeal to you the most?
> 4. List the answers to the above questions. Which five values are the most important to you?
> 5. For each of the values, consider what they mean for you specifically. What behaviors do you believe represent each of the values? How does that show up in your life? Now connect these values to work. How do you see your values turn up at your work? How do your values contribute to your feeling of meaning?

Connect your personal purpose to your work

When your personal purpose is in line with the purpose of the organization, that provides energy and engagement. For example, if you care very much about the environment then you will most certainly want to work for a company with an aligned purpose. If you consider happiness at work important, you will choose a company that puts the happiness of their employees first. Ultimately, those choices will yield more enjoyment, satisfaction, and happiness than a high salary or other benefits. Your values will feel aligned with your work. Therefore, explicitly ask during the job interview what the values of the company are, how they are expressed and how that translates to the daily work.

> **Annie:** *"Once I applied for the job, the HR manager that I spoke with did not really know what the values of the company were. What are you supposed to do if that happens?"*

Actually, that says enough, doesn't it? If an organization focuses on its values, everyone should be able to easily explain what they are and how they are visible in daily life. If you find the HR manager unable to explain them, this would indicate that they are not that important. The same is true for yourself. You must be able to explain what your values are and describe the behavior that fits with your values. If you are clear on your values, then you may expect that from organizations too.

Understand what your purpose means to you and how you can make it practical

If you understand why you do the things you do, how you make a difference, then you are prepared to go the extra mile. It is not always necessary to do 'grand' things to experience a feeling of purpose. It is about making the contributions of your work clear. Every role and function in an organization is a link in the chain, and therefore important. It is important to be able to clearly follow that chain and connect it to the work that you do. You should be aware of it, and reflect on it every now and then. Write it down, share it with others. In the next two weeks, try to make a list at the end of every day of the ways in which you have contributed to the bigger picture. How did you make a difference today? For whom? Just thinking about it is not enough. Writing it down is more effective, because when you make it more explicit you will experience more satisfaction.

> **Eight Ideas to Improve Your Sense of Purpose**
>
> 1. Make a list of people for whom you meant something today and why.
>
> 2. Thank someone today who did something meaningful for you.
>
> 3. Think back to your childhood. What did you want to be as a grown-up and why? Do you recognize that in your current work? What does that mean?
>
> 4. Put something in your purse or your pocket that reminds you of your purpose.
>
> 5. Ask a colleague how they see your added value.

> 6. Find an object at your office that symbolizes the thing that you are most proud of.
>
> 7. What if you do not find purpose in your work? You can also search for something outside your job: coaching a softball team or doing volunteer work, for example.

IMPROVING ON PEOPLE - CONNECTION

The managing director of a medium-sized law firm wanted to put happiness at work on the agenda. This was received with skepticism from her colleagues. Nevertheless, she persevered and used the topic everywhere: it was on the agenda during company and team meetings, and there were discussions and workshops about happiness at work and how to improve it. Part of the initiative was a Christmas box with ten small presents that were all linked to happiness at work, such as chocolate that you could share with colleagues and Christmas cards that were already stamped and addressed to a colleague. As a gift for the entire office, she put a stand with feedback postcards at the front desk. These tools made it very easy for colleagues to surprise each other with a compliment every now and then. One of the lawyers shared her experience: "One day I was in court for a very tough hearing. When I opened my file in the courthouse, there was a handwritten card from my colleague with a message to spur me on. That really lifted me up."

When we talk about happiness at work during workshops, improvement on the 'people' pillar is often on top of the list of good intentions. But which behaviors are needed for more connection?

Start with one of the following:
- Be aware of the effect your behavior has on others.
- Invest in good relationships.

Be aware of the effect your behavior has on others

Whichever mindset you choose, the kind of feedback you give, how you behave during moments that count—all of these have an impact on other people. Your behavior has an immediate influence on others because it determines how they feel. It also has an indirect influence, because people constantly copy other people's behavior. Being aware of that is the first step, only then can you adjust your behavior. It is not the intention of your behavior that counts, but rather the effect of your behavior on others.

Invest in good relationships

A participant in a workshop shared that, when she started her current job, she was determined to show real interest in her colleagues, to be kind and give sincere attention. With tears in her eyes, she told her colleagues: "I now realize that I absolutely am not doing that. I barely say good morning, and I seldom ask any of you how you are doing. I am sorry. From now on I really want to do this differently." In our personal or romantic relationships we often say that you have to 'work on the relationship'. The same applies for work relationships; you must invest in relationships with time and attention. In that sense, relationships at work are no different from romantic relationships or friendships. To build a good relationship it is important that you really pay attention to each other, that you deal with each other's emotions in a respectful and understanding way, that you listen and are open to different opinions—that you try to truly understand each other, and you put yourselves in the other person's position. It is equally important that you do fun things together and take time for small talk, drink a cup of coffee, or have lunch together, that you are prepared to help out in times of need. A social support network at work contributes a lot to our resiliency. If we know that there is someone at work who has our back, that creates a feeling of psychological safety and connectedness. We feel supported, and we perform better.

Ten Ideas to Improve Your Sense of Connection

1. Have a cup of coffee with a colleague every day.

2. Drop a thank you note on the desk of a colleague.

3. Ask about how a colleague's weekend was—be truly interested.

4. Join your colleagues in a hackathon or collecting money for a good cause.

5. Celebrate your birthday with a treat.

6. Celebrate the birthday of your colleague with a surprise: a photo collage of the past year, their favorite cake, or a gift that you made yourself.

7. Organize after work drinks, a party, or to go for coffee and play a silly game.

8. Work out or go for a run or walk together with a colleague.

9. Celebrate all that you can, from the anniversary of the company to the arrival of the Easter bunny. Unexpected surprises usually have the most impact.

10. Did you notice a new colleague? Say: 'Welcome! It's great that you're here! Would you like to join me for lunch today?'

Annie: *"Isn't all of this pretty obvious?"*

It sure is! Most things that we can do to improve our connection with colleagues are self-evident. Sadly, we see that people often forget about it again and again in the madness of the typical work day. When we are very busy, the first thing to go is small talk, which isn't very smart because that's one of our best tools to cultivate good relationships. And good relationships are exactly what you need when you're busy. In spite of knowing what we should do, we often still don't do it.

IMPROVEMENT ON PROGRESS – SATISFACTION

"If you don't know where you're going to, any road will get you there," the Cheshire Cat said to Alice. And that's exactly right. If you want to experience a feeling of progress, you have to know where you want to go.

You can do the following things:
- Make choices;
- Make your results clear;
- Do what you are good at;
- Focus;
- Take breaks in order to increase your productivity.

Make choices

There will always be more work than you can fit into the hours of the day. Have you ever gone home with the feeling that all the work was done? Surely not. There is always something that you would like to have finished. However, not all work is equally important. That means you must make choices. What are the things on your to-do list that are really important and that contribute to achieving your (team) goals? How can you cut them up into manageable pieces? What is the one thing that is the most important[44]? We become more effective by making choices. That also means that there will be things that we do not do.

> **Accountability Call**
>
> Every Monday morning Linda's phone rings at exactly 8:55 a.m. She has a set appointment with her so-called 'accountability partner'. They discuss the focus points of the previous week and how things went. What was successful, what wasn't, and why? What are the three focus points of the coming week? They also discuss how these focus points will contribute to the success of the team and achieving their goals. The points must be concrete, achievable, and with a clear output. "On a regular basis we must be strict with each other: is this truly what is the most important? We have done this for more than two years now and it has become a part of our start of the week ritual. It helps me to maintain focus if someone else is challenging and pushing me. It works better than just having the intention myself. By making a promise to my partner, that accountability makes all the difference."

---

44   Keller, Gary & Papasan, Jay (2013). 1 Ding. Het verrassend simpele idee dat je leven zal veranderen, Xander Uitgevers. Translated by Sandra C. Hessels.

> "THERE CAN ONLY BE ONE MOST IMPORTANT THING. MANY THINGS MAY BE IMPORTANT, BUT ONLY ONE CAN BE THE MOST IMPORTANT."
>
> – ROSS GARBER –

Make your results clear

If at the end of the day you don't know exactly what it was that you have done, that leaves you unfulfilled. This is a common theme; people often do not know where the day has gone, or they never got to the one thing they set out to do that day. There is a simple solution for this: document the work that you have done. One of the participants of a workshop said that she found digital to-do lists very depressing: "If you have done something, you check it off and then it disappears right away! So, I don't know what I have done anymore." That's why she now has a to-do list and a 'tadaaaa' list of completed tasks. "When I try to remember what I have accomplished at the end of the week, I can look back and see all the work that I have achieved. That really feels good! It's also a great tool for 121 reviews, professional development, and annual reviews. You will have a ready-made list to show the work you HAVE accomplished over the year."

Do what you are good at

Doing what you are good at, and what makes you happy, yields a lot: better results, better collaboration. It is important to continue challenging yourself to become even better. Stepping out of your comfort zone every now and then, learning new things, and developing your talents all contribute to your happiness. Do what you enjoy doing, but never stop learning.

> "THE MAGIC STARTS AT THE END OF YOUR COMFORT ZONE."

Focus

Many people complain about a lack of focus, concentration, or being able to think deeply. Research[45] shows that our ability to concentrate has decreased. The story goes that these days we can only be focused on something for eight seconds—that is one second less than the attention span of a goldfish. Even though other studies claim that we never have been able to concentrate for a long time, it appears that increased use of technology has had a negative impact on our ability to focus. The distraction of social media increases exponentially the more we try—and fail—to ignore it. We get addicted to the dopamine shot social media gives us. Cold turkey works best: remove all notifications from your phone and only look at it at set times. There's also no need to continuously check your email; twice a day is usually enough. Block out time in your agenda for deep thinking, and protect that time. Apps such as Forest or the Pomodoro Technique can be helpful for establishing these habits. After thinking deeply for about four hours, your brain is done for the day. This is a good time to work on

---

45 Microsoft Canada (2015). Attention spans: Consumer Insights (report).

tasks for which you don't have to think that deeply[46].

> **Build a Forest**
> Using the Forest app you can indicate how long you want to work without a break—without access to your phone. That can be a short period or a long one, whatever works best for you. During this time period you cannot use your phone. If you allow yourself to be distracted by your phone before the time is up, the virtual tree that you planted in the app at the beginning of the period will die. If you do complete the period, a fully grown tree is added to your forest in the app. The people behind the app will plant a real tree once you reach a certain number of points.

Take breaks to increase your productivity

Do you sometimes think that you are too busy to take a break? Many people (incorrectly) assume this. It turns out that it is very important for our productivity to stop every now and then and give our brain a break. Walk around the block during lunchtime, get up and go to the coffee machine on another floor, or stare out of the window at a tree or a green field. Being out in nature is best, but even looking at a tree or parkland can give you positive benefits. You get more done and it's better for your health.

Annie: "I find it very stressful when I have too much to do. I prefer to stay a few hours after regular work to get it all done. However, my manager says he's not a fan of overtime. He says it's no use because working longer doesn't yield anything. Is that right?"

It is fine to work a little longer every now and then to

---

46   Newport, Cal (2016). Diep werk. Werken in een wereld vol afleiding, Business Contact. Translated by Wybrand Scheffer.

get your work done, in order to go home satisfied. Research at the University of Stanford[47] shows that productivity per hour decreases significantly if the work-week exceeds 50 hours. After the 55 hour mark, productivity falls so much that working longer doesn't yield anything. Regular overtime is also not good for your health because your body doesn't get enough time to recuperate.

Ten Ideas to Improve Your Feeling of Progress

1. In the morning, start with the task you dislike the most.

2. At the end of your workday, make a list of what you have done and what you are going to do tomorrow, listed in order of importance.

3. Take regular breaks, get a cup of coffee, stretch your legs, chat with someone.

4. What new thing have you learned today/this week? Keep track of that for a while.

5. Make a not-to-do list: take your to-do list and choose the five most important points; write those down on a separate list. From those, take the three most important items and write those on another list. All other things go to the not-to-do list.

6. Stop trying to multitask with things that require brain capacity; you are wasting time and energy.

7. For every meeting ask yourself: do I really have to be here or can I spend my time more

---

47   Sullivan, Bob (2015). 'Memo to work martyrs: Long hours make you less productive', Today.com. https://www.cnbc.com/2015/01/26/working-more-than-50-hours-makes-you-less-productive.html. Consulted on May 1, 2020.

> effectively? Choose! And then go for it 100%. This includes not reading emails during the meeting.
>
> 8. Take breaks from social media and email; focus on your work and turn off all your notifications.
>
> 9. Dare to say 'no'.
>
> 10. Are you continuously disturbed by your colleagues while you're in a groove with your work? Agree upon a sign. At Abbvie in Denmark all employees received a plush frog. When that frog lies on the computer that means 'I don't want to be disturbed right now'.

IMPROVEMENT ON POSITIVITY – FUN

Positivity has everything to do with feeling good (mentally) and having energy and vitality, but also with adopting a positive attitude. There is a lot we can do to set ourselves up for success, such as:

- Pay attention to your vitality and energy;
- Set a worry break of 15 minutes;
- Talk more positively;
- Have fun.

Pay attention to your vitality and energy

A healthy diet, sufficient sleep, and the correct balance between effort and relaxation all influence our energy level during the workday. Taking a break on a regular basis, taking a walk while discussing something, eating healthily: these are all things that we can build into our daily patterns. Many people are often tired, and they think that's because they work too hard. A lack of energy, being tired all the time and being exhausted are not necessarily caused by hard work[48], but by not allowing enough time to recharge. It is not the work pressure that causes psychological fatigue, but rather the fact that we do not relax enough—or we try to do it in the wrong way. If we collapse on the couch when we're tired that does not necessarily give us more energy. You would be better off exploring what recharges you and what gives you energy, not just at work but also outside it. This can be sources of energy such as yoga, meditation, or sports that contribute directly to our physical health. It could be a hobby, a good conversation, or taking a walk during lunch.

> **Stress is Useful, but Not Too Much**
>
> A certain level of stress is useful: it boosts our energy and focus. It allows us to function optimally at certain times. Think, for instance, of a time when you had to prepare a slide deck: under a little bit of pressure, this usually goes much quicker than without. Think about the last week before you go on vacation: many people get a tremendous amount of work done. But we cannot do that endlessly. If we are continuously stressed, we become exhausted. And if that lasts too long, we run the risk of burn-out.

Set a worry break of 15 minutes

We are masters at causing—and increasing—unhappiness at work for ourselves by allowing and stimulating negative thoughts, worrying and stressing ourselves out. One way of increasing our happiness at work is by decreasing these 'unhappiness factors'. That will leave more room for happiness and positivity. Do you suffer from worrying? Set aside 15 minutes in your schedule to worry. During this time, you write down everything that you are worried about. Maybe you need to do

---

48   Megens, Jussi (2019). 'We werken niet te veel, we ontspannen te weinig', Carrière.nu. https://carriere.nu/we-werken-niet-te-veel-we-ontspannen-te-weinig. Consulted on May 6, 2020.

this several times a day. After 15 minutes, stop. If another worrying thought pops up in your head, you simply say to yourself: "Not now, wait for the 'worry break'."

Talk more positively

Using positive words makes you feel better, since you focus more on positivity— but this is easier said than done. During the International Week of Happiness at Work in early 2020, alongside our Belgian colleagues, we introduced the no-complaints-for-30-days challenge. One of the participants sent us a text: "I thought I was a pretty positive person, but I already lost on the first day of the challenge! I started over and then I lost again on day three. It is really hard, before you know it you have complained about something. I never thought it would be that difficult. But I'm going to try again. #persevere." Changing your language as a challenge exercise would be a great start for many people. Just by keeping track of how many positive and negative words and sentences you use in one day will raise your awareness significantly. You can then teach yourself new behavior. Make sure you do this together with your colleagues. Language is contagious: if you complain, others will also complain. If you speak negatively about others, then others will do that too. The reverse is true also: if you take a positive and proactive position, then others are more inclined to follow suit. Therefore, if you do this together, you will have more impact.

Have fun

Having fun is important in experiencing happiness at work. Just be silly at work once in a while—involve your colleagues too! For example, designate a 'dancing zone' somewhere and post a sign with the text: 'Forbidden to walk here, only dancing is allowed.' Agree with your colleagues to all dress in a certain color on Fridays. Post a joke in the elevator every week. Use tape to make a hopscotch track on the floor in the corridor. Agree to all wear a Christmas sweater the day before Christmas, etc…

Ten Ideas to Experience More Positivity

1. Write down what you are grateful for every day. Share it with your colleagues, for instance via a chat channel or on a whiteboard in the coffee area.

2. Allow yourself some space to make jokes during work; that is not a waste of time.

3. When something goes wrong: laugh about it and solve it.

4. Celebrate your success!

5. Mind your language: positive words have a positive effect.

6. Do work that you enjoy doing.

7. Move during your workday. For instance, get up every hour, walk up and down the stairs, and then continue with what you were doing. Make moving a set part of your daily routine.

8. Organize a league in ping pong/darts/throwing wads of paper into the wastebasket.

9. You can do yoga even behind your desk. Really. Google it.

10. Play complaint/positivity bingo with your colleagues: a bingo card with the most heard complaining sentences and positive sentences. Do you hear one of those sentences? You can scratch that off. Who will have bingo first?

JUST TRY IT

Now you know what to do to take ownership and develop a growth mindset. You also know how to design behavioral change and what you should do for more happiness at work. The next step is to actually do it! If you want to change something, it doesn't need to be perfect right away. Just try it. If you are not successful in keeping up your new behavior, then look at the different steps: what can you change? Then try it again. If you start changing your behavior with a sense of ownership and a growth mindset, it will happen for you.

CHAPTER 9
THE MANAGER AND A POSITIVE TEAM CULTURE

In the previous chapters you have read what happiness at work actually is, why it is so important, and what every employee can do to increase their own happiness at work. If you are a manager you have the power to contribute to the happiness of your team as well as your own personal happiness. Our research shows that managers play a big part in how happy their employees are at work[49]: 63% of respondents in this survey indicated that their happiness at work was determined by their immediate manager, the management team, or the board of directors. In their article, Allas and Schaninger of McKinsey state that bosses and superiors play a bigger part in contentment at work and the wellbeing of employees than they realize[50].

---

49   MonitorGroep (2019). Werkgeluk in Nederland. https://happyoffice.nl/werkgeluk-onderzoek-2019. Consulted on January 10, 2022. 2

50   Allas en Schaninger (2020) The Boss factor: Making the world a better place through workplace relationships, McKinsey Quaterly, McKinsey.com https://www.mckinsey.com/business-functions/people-and-organizational-performance/our-insights/the-boss-factor-making-the-world-a-better-place-through-workplace-relationships. Consulted on January 10, 2022

There has even been research[51][52], showing that employees quit more often because of their manager than because of the work itself. While employees are primarily responsible for their own happiness at work, as a manager or leader you also have a huge influence on your team's or organization's happiness levels. So, as a leader, how can you help people take ownership? How can you stimulate a growth mindset within the team? How can you focus on the four pillars of happiness at work? How do you contribute to a positive work culture as a leader and manager?

THE MINDSET OF A MANAGER

A few years ago, Maartje was watching her son's soccer match: "I did that almost every Saturday, and as you do, you get talking to other parents while you watch. One of these days, I had an interesting conversation with one of the fathers. As the owner of a car dealership he was managing a team, and he shared with me that he really hated it. He said he would prefer to just sell the whole company because he found the management of people very stressful. According to him, his employees were lazy, they took stuff home that didn't belong to them, and he thought it was his primary task to check on them at all times. It was literally killing him. He gave me a summarized description of his medical history. As well as severe burnout, he had also suffered a number of strokes. In short, his role as manager didn't make him very happy." This soccer dad's story stuck with me, and was quite different from another manager I spoke to not long after that. The owner of Aldowa, a construction company that specializes in cladding, had a totally different image of his employees than the car dealership manager. For him the key was trust. He told me: 'When people receive trust, they are part of it. Sometimes I hear people say that trust must be earned. But I think that is backwards. If you start working somewhere, do you really want to start from a position of mistrust? I certainly wouldn't.' These are the stories of

---

51 Hyacinth, Brigette (2017). 'Employees don't leave Companies, they leave Managers', LinkedIn.com. https://www.linkedin.com/pulse/employees-dont-leave-companies-managers-brigette-hyacinth. Consulted on May 10, 2020.

52 Bradberry, Travis (2016). '9 Things That Make Good Employees Quit', Forbes. https://www.forbes.com/sites/travisbradberry/2016/02/23/9-things-that-make-good-employees-quit/#430b20d11b83. Consulted on May 10, 2020.

two managers, and two extremes in how they view their employees, experience their work, and bring their own viewpoint to their role."

The difference between managers X and Y

Back in 1960, American management professor Douglas McGregor developed a theory about organizations and management in which two opposite human images take center stage: human image X and human image Y. The human image that you as a manager have—consciously or subconsciously—determines your style of management. It influences how you regard work, how you direct and motivate people, and how much space you leave for the responsibility and creativity of your coworkers.

Human image X

X-managers have a pessimistic human image. In their eyes, people are lazy by nature and try to avoid working as much as possible. They have no ambitions, want as little responsibility as possible, and want to be told exactly what to do. X-managers are convinced that people will do all that they can to avoid working, and that you can only motivate them with financial stimuli or punishment. This perceived laziness is why X-managers feel it is necessary to force people to work and to check up on them all the time. According to X-managers, the system of rewarding and punishing works best. They also think it is necessary to record exactly which tasks a person has to complete and how those tasks must be executed. An autocratic leadership style, sharp control, and hierarchical principles are cornerstones of this type of leadership. The biggest problem of X-management is that it often leads to a culture of fear.

Human image Y

Compared to X-managers, managers with the human image Y have an optimistic view of their people. They assume that people are intrinsically motivated to work, to reach their goals, and to contribute to something bigger than themselves. They believe that work gives meaning, satisfaction, appreciation, and enjoyment to their people. Y-managers assume that employees need autonomy and responsibility. They see that a system of rewarding and punishing is not the way to stimulate people to work. Y-managers prefer a democratic or facilitating style of management, and allow people a lot of freedom. Employees are given the chance to develop, and to work to—and with—their strengths.

What type of manager do you want to be?

The examples of Maartje's conversations illustrate how human images X and Y are almost diametrically opposed. The soccer father clearly regarded his fellow human beings with suspicion, while the owner of Aldowa chose to trust his people. This theory offers a good starting point to look at your own convictions and beliefs as a manager, and how those affect your style of management and your behavior. Based on those insights you can then decide what kind of manager you would like to be, and what you might need to change in your attitude and your behavior. The following diagram shows the differences between X- and Y-managers.

X-manager (Pessimistic)	Aspect	Y-manager (Optimistic)
Employees are lazy and only work to make money	Attitude regarding work	Employees love to work and want to contribute and achieve goals
Command & Control micro-management	Management	Autonomy and responsibility, facilitating and coaching
People's nature is to avoid responsibility	Responsibility	People want responsibility
Management by fear (punishment and rewards)	Motivation	Employees are intrinsically motivated

X-manager (Pessimistic)	Aspect	Y-manager (Optimistic)
Managers are creative, do the thinking, have oversight, therefore they direct tasks for employees to execute	Creativity	Every human being is creative and by means of autonomy you can utilize this potential

> **Exercise: What is Your Human Image?**
>
> Consider how you think about your people. Keep a journal for a while and write down how you view the employees in your team.
>
> What is your opinion about:
> 1. their attitude towards work;
> 2. the management that is required;
> 3. how much responsibility they take;
> 4. their motivation;
> 5. their creativity.
>
> Attention: this exercise is intended as a reflection on your own convictions, rather than passing judgment on your employees. Keep this in mind and write down your perceptions of employees. So, not "Pete is barely doing what he needs to do," or: "Marie doesn't need direction, she can work by herself," but: "I catch myself thinking that Pete doesn't like his work and that he therefore barely does the minimum," or: "I don't feel that Marie needs direction." The more situations you describe, the more complete your reflection will be. Then draw a five-point scale for each aspect of the X-manager and Y-manager. Indicate on these scales where you think that you

> are, per situation (or per day). At the end of the period, take a look at where you are most of the time. Which human image are you inclined towards? And how does that reflect in the behavior of your employees? What would you like to change about that?

Influence on culture

It is interesting that both X and Y managers often see their human image confirmed. For instance an X-manager, like the soccer father, imposes many rules and checks on his people from his conviction that employees are lazy and only work to make money. As a result, this makes people passive and supports a wait-and-see attitude which in turn confirms his image of his employees. On the other hand, Y-managers give their employees responsibilities which increases their autonomy, makes them more loyal, and encourages them to show ownership and take more initiative. It will be clear that Y leadership suits you better if you want to create a positive work culture.

WHAT MAKES A GOOD LEADER?

In 2009, leadership consultancy Zenger-Folkman surveyed 60,000 people regarding what they considered to be good leadership[53]. The two most important criteria turned out to be result orientation and social skills. Result orientation refers to analytical skills in combination with the drive to solve problems and to see progress. Social skills refers to good communication, relationships and empathic ability. 14% of respondents considered a result-oriented leader a good leader, and 12% thought someone with good social skills was a good leader. This result was surprising, considering those were the two most important criteria. However, leaders who combine result orientation with social skills do score high: no less than 72% of respondents considered people with both these skills to be good leaders. A sad note in real life is that just 1% of all leaders score high on both aspects.

---

53   Bradberry, Travis (2016). 'Result Or People: Where Should A Leader Focus?', Forbes. https://www.forbes.com/sites/travisbradberry/2016/12/23/results-or-people-which-deserves-a-leaders-attention/#346d7efe626c. Consulted on March 3, 2020.

Good leadership is about developing a broad palette of skills. It is also important to consider what is needed in your organization or team. And maybe the most important thing: what kind of manager would you like to be and what would be a good way to shape that?

> **Our Brain Develops Like a Seesaw**
>
> The fact that leaders are either result-oriented or relationship-oriented is caused by the fact that our brain finds it difficult to function on both analytical and social elements at the same time. Our brain consists, as it were, of two networks that are connected to each other like a seesaw. When one network develops, the other one develops less. Traditionally, result-orientation and analytical thinking was more valued for leaders, and therefore more attention was paid to developing the analytical part of the brain[54].

The difference between a leader and a manager

Another thing that can be an obstacle for good leadership is the emotional meaning of the concepts of 'manager' and 'leader'. A manager is a person who oversees an existing situation and focuses on goals, agreements, procedures, and results. A leader directs change, renewal, and innovation based on a vision of the future; they encourage people by taking the lead so that others can follow[55]. For most people, 'being a good leader' sounds more heroic than 'being a good manager'. For that reason, many prefer to be seen as a leader rather than a manager. At the same time there will be few people who refer to themselves in daily life as a leader. Imagine you meet your team for the first time and you say,

---

54   Lieberman, Matthew (2013). 'Should Leaders Focus on Results, or on People?', Harvard Business Review. https://hbr.org/2013/12/should-leaders-focus-on-results-or-on-people. Consulted on March 3, 2020.

55   Braun, Thomas (2015). '"Een manager is nog geen leider"', mt Next Leadership Generation. https://www.mt.nl/management/een-manager-is-nog-geen-leider/87966. Consulted on May 22, 2020.

"Hello, I am your new leader." Chances are that you will be made fun of. Whereas if you said, "Hello, I am your new manager," that would be completely acceptable. However, we are comparing apples and oranges. 'Manager' is a job title, while 'leader' is a personal characteristic. Anybody can be a leader, depending on your attitude.

> *Annie: "Just how satisfied are people with their manager?"*

From our research into happiness at work in the Netherlands, the answers show that more than half of the participants (59%) think that they have a good or very good manager, 24% say that they are partly satisfied/not satisfied at all with their manager, and 2% had no opinion. Other research shows that 75% of the interviewees think that the most stressful aspect of their job is dealing with their immediate supervisor.

Other forms of directing

If 'manager' is a job title, you could wonder to what extent this function is needed. More and more organizations are choosing to no longer appoint managers because they think that their employees are very capable of leading themselves. Self-management, informal, and coaching leadership are some of the other ways that are being chosen to ensure that a team, department, or organization can flourish[56]. At Aldowa, for instance, they do not appoint managers. According to the owner of the company, the job title only distracts people while it should actually be about working together, facilitating, inspiring, coaching, and asking questions. Informally, they have leaders—those who already listen to what's on people's minds and who take the lead when things must be done, for instance by coming in 15 minutes earlier to prepare for the day, and by guiding newcomers. These are the people who

---

56   Stewart, Henri (2019). '16 Companies That Don't Have Managers', Happy. co.uk. https://www.happy.co.uk/blogs/16-companies-that-don-t-have-managers. Consulted on May 22, 2020.

signal when something goes wrong and connect people in order to solve the problem. According to the owner, you can only take on this role if you participate actively. In his experience, the moment you make it formal and give this role a job title, that is when things go wrong. Gallup's research shows that globally only 21% of employees are engaged, 19% are actively dis-engaged, and the rest are somewhere in between. The owner of Aldowa believes that engagement is all about taking ownership and responsibility. He says, "Everybody wants responsibility. One maybe more than the other, but I have never met a person who doesn't want any responsibility at all. People are proud when they contribute to the results of the team or organization. If you, as an employer, take your people seriously, then they will take you, their work, clients, and colleagues seriously too. Then they will automatically be engaged and passionate."

Facilitative leadership

There is a lot of buzz about 'facilitative' or 'servant' leadership these days. A facilitative leadership style contributes to happiness at work in many ways. Facilitative leadership style leaders see their role as in service to their people, their organizations, their clients, and the world. By practicing this type of leadership they fulfill different roles, depending on the situation. A facilitative leadership style is geared to what employees need in order to grow and flourish, and encourages autonomy and ownership. In creating more happiness at work, autonomy is one of the most important ingredients.

Purpose and values are important pillars, and because of mutual dependency between leader and employees, personal connection is valued. However, there is also a hidden danger with these leadership styles. Servant leaders can feel inclined to take care of people, and take responsibility for inspiring and making employees engaged and enthused. This is an impossible task, and can lead to employees leaning back and waiting until they are facilitated in the right way. Facilitative leadership can also lead to avoiding unpopular decisions. If facilitative leadership takes that direction, it will be clear that it will not lead to more happiness at work.

HOW WILL YOU GET TO WORK WITH YOUR TEAM?

Your behavior as a leader or manager has a massive impact on the culture in your team. To create a happier team at work you have to put the topic (of happiness at work) firmly on the agenda and start to work with your team on it. The first step is to take a basic measurement: where are we now? How do we feel? The question you should ask is not only, "How happy are you at this moment?" but, "How do you feel today and what contributes most to that feeling?" We need to delve deeper because the first question focuses too much on the feeling of happiness. If you ask this question often without exploring what is behind it, it might cause 'happiness at work' to become an obligation, a must-have, or something that is 'bad' if you do not have it. That is not what we are aiming for. By deepening the questions you inquire about a wide range of emotions that people can experience, and you link that to possible causes. By asking these questions on a regular basis and keeping track of the answers, you—as a leader or manager—and your employees get a better picture about what makes every individual person and the team happy, and what leads to unhappiness. What can you be working on to create a better working environment? Once you have this starting point, then you can delve deeper into the answers by asking specific questions about purpose, people, progress, and positivity. The personal Happiness at Work circle from chapter 8 is a great tool for this.

By taking stock of where you are in terms of your team's happiness at work, you have already started the conversation about Happiness at Work. The next step is to continue the conversation and discuss what happiness at work is, what the scientific backgrounds are, why it is important, and what it can yield for you collectively. Based on the outcomes of your discussions, you can then make a concrete plan of action together. How will you put happiness at work into practice? Your team members need to take ownership and feel responsible for the plan and the outcomes; they should feel free to experiment. You do not build a positive work culture with an exact project plan on paper. It is about doing activities, trying out new ideas, figuring out what works and what doesn't work, and then continue to build on what works.

Handling resistance[57]

Even though happiness at work and building a positive work culture don't seem to be subjects that people would be opposed to, we do experience resistance every now and then. There are several reasons why people don't want to engage with happiness at work. Sometimes people are afraid that the subject hits too close to home, that it is an 'excuse' or a 'trick', and that they will be saddled with extra tasks and duties. We also notice that resistance presents itself in different forms. There is passive resistance, where people just sit through it silently and express themselves nonverbally to indicate that they don't like it. Then there is active resistance where someone expresses themselves explicitly in an unpleasant way. What can you do when people criticize publicly and say things such as, "I'm already very happy, I don't need this at all," "This is such baloney, it doesn't work anyway," or "appiness is something personal, my boss has nothing to do with it"? Whichever form of resistance you encounter, the first two questions you need to ask yourself are: are you convinced of someone's good intentions, and are you truly prepared to understand the other person? Resistance is not a character trait, but it is a reaction by someone to a situation, to something that has gone wrong at some stage. Often the resistance is related to a situation that they are in, or their relationship with you or the team. The subject itself can play a role too. The reaction is a call for attention to something underlying that you should discuss. If you ignore the passive or active resistance, it will continue to smolder beneath the surface. By starting a conversation about it, asking questions, you will ease the resistance. Only then will there be room for change. We give you three ways to handle resistance:

1. Reflective Listening[58]

Resistance can be a way of hiding emotions or needs. If that is the case, your best option is to start with reflective listening. The underlying conviction is that every person has good intentions, and that you should first aim to understand before you can be understood. Start by letting the other person

---

57   Speksnijder, Arie (n.d.). Handout Reflectief luisteren, Bridge2learn.
58   Ibid

explain what bothers them and then summarize what they said. Suppose that someone is upset because they think working on Happiness at Work will only lead to more tasks on their already full plate. You can respond to that by saying, "So you are bummed because increasing happiness at work creates extra workload for you." Or you could choose to reframe their message. Reframing is a special way of reflection where you package the resistance in other words and give new meaning to the statement of the other person. The most effective reframing of resistance is to name the need (the desire) behind the resistance. So when someone says: "I don't believe in happiness at work, it's just a trick to save money by the management team," you could reframe this into: "It is important for you that we are open, transparent, and honest about why we are focussing on happiness at work."

2. Confirming autonomy

When people are forced to do something—even when it is something they actually want to do— resistance is often the automatic response. In these situations, it helps to explicitly emphasize the autonomy of the other person. This can remove a large part of their resistance. You could respond, for instance, by saying, "Because of my enthusiasm about happiness at work it seems like this is something we must do, but I don't want to force anybody to do anything. You are all able to choose for yourself whether you participate or not."

3. Amplified reflection of the resistance

When the resistance is greater or when team members ignore their own responsibility, the tactic of amplified reflection may work. This comes down to repeating the resistance of the others and exaggerating it a bit. Someone may say: "I'm already very happy, I don't see the need to focus on happiness at work." If using this technique, you could say: "So, you see no opportunity to improve anything about your happiness at work?" Or: "So, happiness at work is useless for you." The goal of this action is that the other person may reduce their resistance, creating space to start a discussion about what might be possible.

THE NEXT STEP

How you embody your role as a leader or manager is a big influence on your team culture. Now you know how your own mindset plays a role, and what facilitative leadership can add to this. You know where you can start, how you place the topic on the agenda, and how to handle resistance. The next step is to deepen your own role further, guided by the pillars of happiness at work.

CHAPTER 10

THE MANAGER OR LEADER AND THE FOUR PILLARS OF HAPPINESS AT WORK

When creating a positive team culture—as a manager or leader—you play different parts using the four pillars: 'purpose', 'people', 'progress', and 'positivity'. Below we illustrate how you can use each of the four pillars.

CONTRIBUTING TO PURPOSE – MEANING

As a manager you can contribute to the 'purpose' pillar in three specific ways:

1. Translate the organizational purpose to your team;
2. Start a discussion about the team purpose;
3. Use storytelling.

Translate the organizational purpose for your team

The vision, mission, and purpose of the organization become relevant for your team when you all work together to translate them to your team's contribution, values, and behaviors. The focal question for you here is: how do we, as a group, contribute to the goals of the organization? You can record this with the help of a manifesto. (Read more about how to create a manifesto in the next chapter.) Don't make the mistake of wanting to do this alone, then informing the rest of the team about it. That approach won't work; this process should be done collaboratively.

Start a discussion about the team purpose

When you have translated the organizational purpose into your team purpose and created a manifesto, or written down the main points, it is important to keep the subject alive and to discuss everybody's individual purpose and role on a regular basis. The goal of having conversations about this is to make the contribution, needs, and wishes of all the team members insightful and specific, so that you can divide tasks and responsibilities based on that (and not just based on formal job descriptions).

Nine Questions About Team Purpose

The following questions are good starting points for a discussion about meaning and purpose with your team:

1. How do we, as a team, contribute to the organizational goals and results?

2. For whom do we make a difference?

3. What is everybody's role when we look at the job descriptions?

4. Which (informal) contribution does every member provide to the team?

5. Which team is an inspiring example for you

and why?

6. What is your biggest dream; what would you like to accomplish as a team?

7. What do you consider to be the most important in your work?

8. Why do you work for this organization?

9. What are you most proud of at work?

Use storytelling

In order to make the team's purpose more specific, it helps to tell stories about it. The more visual and personal the stories are, the better they connect with the experience of your team members, and the better they can connect with the purpose. When you get to work with happiness at work and purpose, it is important that you—as a manager—tell your own story: what is your personal purpose, why do you consider happiness at work important, and what do you want to achieve with it? In the next chapter, centered around building a positive organizational culture, we will dive deeper into the subject of storytelling.

Seven Ideas to Strengthen the Team Purpose

There are many appealing things that you can do to increase the sense of purpose in your team.

Here are a few examples:

1. Post pictures of your clients (for whom do you make a difference?).

2. All team members spend a day at work with a client or customer.

3. Tell stories about how clients experience the

> added value of the team (after having spent a day with the client).
>
> 4. Put the team purpose as a fixed item on the agenda and share the (personal) stories about when you experience purpose at work.
>
> 5. Create a purpose wall with memories of meaningful moments.
>
> 6. Visualize your purpose in the work environment, for instance by making a poster or a paper flag line.
>
> 7. Share your team purpose on (internal) communication platforms, so that other teams also know what you stand for.

CONTRIBUTING TO PEOPLE – CONNECTION

Hannah works as a sales manager at a hotel in Amsterdam, and the main reason that she likes working there is her manager. "I started working here because I like to feel at home at work. That means that I feel comfortable with the company policy and that I get along well with my colleagues. But the most important thing for me is the relationship with my manager. That person must be someone who inspires me, whom I trust and who trusts me. That way I can get the best out of myself. When I applied for a job here, it was immediately clear to me that my manager fit the bill." The wishes that Hannah has concerning her work and her manager are recognizable. Nice colleagues and a good relationship with your manager are important for happiness at work. At the same time, we see that working together is not always easy. A negative atmosphere or a complaining culture in a team can be the cause that people feel unhappy at work. To what extent can you, as a manager, influence the connection and atmosphere in your team, and more importantly, how do you put this into practice? How do you contribute to the 'people' pillar as a manager?

Three things are important here:
1. Working on psychological safety;
2. Building an atmosphere of mutual trust;
3. Discouraging dramatic and ego-driven behavior.

Work on psychological safety

Google's research on excellent teams is extensive[59]. They researched 180 teams and conducted more than 200 interviews to discover what makes an effective team. One of the most interesting results of that research reveals that it is not the team of the highest individual performers that accomplishes the most, but the team that works best together. The relationships people have with each other—the group's standards—is what makes the group excellent. The five group standards that are determinative for this are:

1. Psychological safety: team members feel safe to take risks and be vulnerable in front of each other;
2. Dependability: team members get things done on time and meet Google's high bar for excellence;
3. Structure & clarity: team members have clear goals, plans and roles
4. Meaning: work is personally important to team members;
5. Impact: team members think their work matters and creates change.

Research also shows that of these five values, psychological safety is by far the most important. Therefore, if you, as a manager, want to work on more connection, start with working on psychological safety. You can do that in three steps:

1. Making clear agreements

As a leader or manager, bring up the subject of psychological safety in your team and start discussing with each other what

---

59   Edmondson, Amy C. (2019). De onbevreesde organisatie, Business Contact. Translated by Albert Witteveen.

that means for each of you. How do you deal with each other in a safe environment? What does that look like and what do each of you need? It is important to also clearly explain the relevance of psychological safety and what everybody gains from it. Based on these conversations, make clear agreements with each other about which behavior you think is acceptable and which is not. For instance, how do you address each other? What do you do when there are complaints or gossip? How much space do you allow each other to make sure everybody has their say? How do you deal with making mistakes and vulnerability? To what extent do you respect each other's time, and do you honor your agreements?

2. Setting a good example

Once agreements regarding behavior are clear, then as a manager you need to set the right example. It helps to explicitly invite people to join in. Just explaining why psychological safety is important and making agreements about what that looks like is not enough to actually change team behavior. This is especially true if the sense of psychological safety needs to be (re)built because of past experiences. Ask people to express themselves and start doing that yourself. Taking the first step by allowing yourself to be vulnerable and showing the desired behavior will eventually help others to (dare to) follow.

3. Respond in a positive way

Creating a psychologically safe environment is a learning process; Allow people time and space to learn. In order to learn new behavior people must be able to practice it, remembering that practice doesn't always go well the first few times. It is important—and this also applies to other managers in the organization—that you respond positively, even when mistakes are made. Only when you structurally encourage the desired behavior, will you build a psychologically safe environment in a sustainable way.

Building mutual trust

While psychological safety is about group level collaboration within the bigger picture, trust is about interaction between individuals. How do you create trust between yourself and your employees? Do you start with trust, and give someone space from day one, or do you prefer to loosen the reins gradually? To what extent can you influence mutual trust between team members? Your attitude as a manager and the example that you set, consciously or subconsciously, determines whether you are creating an environment of mutual trust. Starting with mistrust until the opposite has been proven is an uncomfortable starting point, so start off on the right foot. Building trust takes time, and is created by the positive experiences you have together. Make sure that you are creating an environment where having positive experiences together happens from day one. Listen very carefully to your employees, communicate openly, and be aware of what's going on in your team.

Discourage dramatic and ego-driven behavior

Research[60] shows that people spend two and a half hours per day—almost a third of the workday—on behavior that doesn't contribute to achieving results. This behavior includes negative emotions in the form of dramatic or ego-driven behavior: complaining, nagging, judging, gossiping, venting, etc. This type of behavior affects the psychological safety and the mutual trust between employees. As a manager, it is your task to stop this. One way of doing that is by focusing on the facts. When someone comes to you with a complaint, when they're venting or gossiping, don't react to the complaint itself. Instead, search for facts and solutions together with the person concerned. Ask questions like "What do you know for sure about this problem?", "What are the facts?", "What is your part in this?", "What are your ideas for a solution and what have you already done to help?" With these types of questions, the thinking process shifts from emotions to facts. If you do this consistently, the employees themselves will learn how to follow this process. This increases the likelihood that, instead of bringing complaints to you, they will go straight to their colleague and offer their help, or come to you with a solution to check, which benefits the building of mutual trust and collaboration.

---

60 Wakeman, Cy (2017). No Ego: How Leaders Can Cut the Cost of Workplace Drama, End Entitlement, and Drive Big Results, St. Martin's Press.

What Does Your Ideal Working Situation Look Like?

Andrea, a friend of ours, works as a manager at a large governmental agency. One of her employees came into her office and sighed deeply. When Andrea asked what was wrong, her employee started off by saying, "I feel ignored by everybody, in my work. I don't have clearly defined responsibilities and I don't know what my role in the team is anymore."

Instead of disproving the words of her employee, telling her how good she is, or offering solutions for her problems, Andrea asks, "What does a great job look like for you? What is your role and what do you do?"

The employee looked surprised, thought for a moment and then replied: "That I have clear structure in my work and actually in my whole life. That I am in touch with people, and I know what everybody is doing."

"Great," Andrea answered. "What have you done already to make this come true and what else can you do?" Her employee thought again and said, "I could chat more often with my colleagues and plan a lunch date every week." They both agreed that this was a good start.

The employee went back to work, feeling much more positive. When we discussed this with Andrea, she said, "Before, I used to come up with solutions that worked for me when people came in with these types of questions, but of course, that doesn't help them. In fact, I sometimes make the problem bigger instead of smaller. But now by asking my colleague to come up with solutions themselves, they get better ideas that truly help them.

When Andrea came up with the solution herself, and by asking the right questions, not giving answers, I was able to really help her." This is exactly right. Stopping ego-driven behavior means having the right conversation and asking the right questions.

Seven Ideas to Improve the 'People' Pillar

What can you do to increase the sense of connection in your team?

1. Be clear about behavior that is and is not tolerated.

2. Do not let undesirable behavior go unnoticed; intervene when people don't adhere to the agreements.

3. Hire 'nice' people and involve your team with recruitment and the selection of new team members.

4. Have conversations on a regular basis about 'rumors'. Ask employees if they have heard any rumors recently that they are curious about. Then tell the real story.

5. Give new employees a warm welcome by ensuring an unforgettable first day at work. This means going beyond operational basics like making sure there is a desk, that all the technical stuff works, and that all necessary facilities are present. Put together a welcome pack and do something playful, like receiving the new employee with a standing ovation from the entire team.

6. Have colleagues praise each other and reward that with a gift card, paid for by the organization.

7. Many people love having a team day

> together. Playing a game, like Personality Poker, can make it even more fun. Plus you get to know each other even better and get to share what makes each of you happy at work. More information on personalitypokergame.com

CONTRIBUTING TO PROGRESS – RESULTS

When Tiger Woods was seven years old, his father would take him to the golf course on a regular basis and ask him, "Where would you like to hit the ball?" The young Woods would pick out a spot and then his father just said, "Great, now figure out how to do it." He didn't give Tiger any tips, didn't tell him how to do it. There was no advice on how to adjust his arm the right way or where to place his feet. He kept it simple; set a goal together with his son, asked him how he wanted to achieve that goal and then let the boy figure it out for himself[61].

For employees, seeing the results of their own work and personal development contributes to satisfaction and happiness at work. Your role as a manager is to create the right conditions for this and, just like Tiger Woods' father, let people do as much as they can themselves. As a manager you can contribute in the following ways to the 'progress' pillar:

1. Give employees autonomy within clearly defined guide lines and call them out on their ownership;
2. Give your employees good (growth) feedback and help them develop a growth mindset;
3. Make results visible and don't forget to celebrate them;
4. Help employees to work in flow.

Give autonomy within clear guidelines

Autonomy is about how people decide for themselves how they will achieve their goals and how they want to shape their

---

61 Shambora, Jessica (2009). 'Best advice I ever got', Fortune.com. https://archive.fortune.com/galleries/2009/fortune/0906/gallery.best_advice_i_ever_got2.fortune/index.html. Consulted on February 26, 2020.

work. Research[62] shows that when people must choose between complete freedom when doing their work, or freedom within clear guidelines, the majority choose the latter. Therefore, it is important for a manager to set clear guidelines, to give people autonomy within those guidelines and then offer the support that they need.

Two things are needed to create a clear framework:
1. the principles, values, and norms of the organization; how we act on behalf of our company;
2. the organizational goals; how do we contribute to those goals as a team and as individual team members and what do we specifically agree upon about that?

For instance, you can let people determine their working hours themselves. To have freedom within clear guidelines to decide which times they work, the teams will need to coordinate with each other what work needs to be done and by when, and to decide for themselves which meetings they should or should not attend. These guidelines are important to ensure that there is clarity, which creates the freedom within which your employees can work.

Give good (growth) feedback

Good feedback is important for happiness at work. It contributes to experiencing progress, both in work and in respect to someone's personal development. Therefore, feedback needs to be a set part of both of these processes. As a manager, it's part of your role to make clear the agreements with your team and your employees about the frequency, timing, and the form of feedback that you give each other. It is also important that in your role as manager you focus on growth feedback: feedback about the process and the steps that people take. That way you not only help people in their task-related and personal development, but also in stimulating their growth mindset.

---

62   Stewart, Henry (2012). The Happy Manifesto: Make Your Organization a Great Workplace, Happy.

Annie: *"Earlier in the book you said that a growth mindset greatly influences happiness at work. But what can you do with that as a manager?"*

Research by Marloes van Hoeve[63] shows that teachers have a great influence on the mindset of students in regards to mathematics. During the research, students were first given a short questionnaire. Their teacher then provided instruction on mindset, neuroplasticity, making mistakes, and feedback. Throughout the process, the teacher led by example by demonstrating their own positive growth mindset. Through short assignments, the students were then invited to develop their own growth mindsets and consider its impact upon their work. Afterwards, the students filled out another questionnaire. The result? After the intervention they showed a growth mindset more often than before the intervention. One of the most important conclusions drawn from this work was that the teacher and their mindset has a lot of influence on the mindset of their students. You can translate that influence to organizations. Managers, their mindset, and the way in which they give feedback can help employees to think more from a growth mindset. By taking this into account, for instance during appraisals or in meetings, you can achieve a lot.

Six Tips for Giving Better Feedback

When feedback is given, both the giver and the receiver often feel vulnerable. To make sure that it will be a good and pleasant conversation, these tips can be helpful:

- First check and see if a person is open to

---

63   Hoeve, Marloes van (n.d.). https://www.uu.nl/onderzoek/onderzoek-op-scholen/afgeronde-onderzoeken/marloes-van-hoeve. Consulted on May 12, 2020.

your feedback.

- Give growth feedback, i.e. feedback about things that a person can change (focus on process instead of characteristics). Review the tips about growth feedback from chapter 6.

- Keep your feedback narrow in scope and describe specific behavior that you have seen. Only use examples that you have experienced yourself, so say things like 'I see' and 'I hear'. Avoid words like 'never' and 'always'.

- To avoid sounding confrontational, speak in the first person and steer clear of judgment or expressing your own opinion. For example, you could say: "I find it hard to tell my story if you keep interrupting me," instead of: "You keep interrupting me and I find that irritating."

- Allow space to comprehend and to react. Also check this with questions such as: "Do you recognize this?" "Do you think this is correct?"

- Offer a specific tip to do things differently or come up with a solution together.

Make results visible and celebrate them

A team at a Danish pension fund had a large backlog in entering pension policies into the system. No matter what methods the team used in an attempt to get caught up, nothing worked. Every week more policies were added than were processed. Finally, during a meeting, someone came up with the idea to look at the total number of policies that had to be processed that month to get back on schedule. That number turned out to be 1,000. They stopped focusing on the backlog and instead went to work with a new goal: entering 1,000 policies into the system. Immediately, the energy returned, and at the end of every workday the end total was written on the whiteboard. It quickly emerged that this approach worked. In fact, it surpassed all expectations. By the 17th of the month the team surpassed their monthly goal total of 1,000 policies. The team was so energized by their progress that they continued to count. When there was no more room on the whiteboard, a piece of paper was attached above the board to keep track of the numbers. Focusing on results, making them visible, and celebrating them affects people's motivation a lot. As a manager, it is a good idea to take the lead on this and celebrate the work you and your team have achieved, rather than focussing solely on the work yet to be completed.

Help employees to work in flow

Cynthia Maxwell was working as a Director of Engineering at Yahoo when—according to her—she made a big mistake. She had convinced a previous colleague to come work for her on an important project, but after a few months the programmer decided to return to his previous employer. Working at Yahoo was not what he had expected. He did not feel challenged enough and did not think that he could develop sufficiently at Yahoo.

Maxwell could have kicked herself. She had been so engrossed with the details of the project that she had completely missed the fact that one of her most talented employees was not happy. She did not want to experience this ever again, so she decided to do things differently. She searched for a way to get better insights on the emotions of employees and came up with a tool to convert those emotions into data. For this she was inspired by the principle of flow, the brainchild of Mihaly Csikszentmihalyi[64].

As we explained in chapter 3, flow is the right balance between challenge and skills. If, like Maxwell, you are seeking to increase flow for your employees in their work, then you should start by monitoring this balance. You might choose to have one-to-one conversations with your employees to ask them how they are doing professionally. Ask them to place a

---

64   Csikszentmihalyi, Mihaly (2020). Flow. Psychologie van de optimale ervaring, Ten Have.

dot on a chart where the one axis is 'challenge' and the other one is 'skills' (see figure). Mark the area where skills and challenges are in balance; this is where people experience flow. When people choose a dot above the path of flow, it is a sign that they are experiencing tension and that something needs to happen to lower the challenge and/or to increase the skills.

When people indicate that they are below the path of flow, that indicates boredom. Discuss with them how more challenges can be created in their work. As long as people are on the path of flow things are fine, unless employees always place the dot on the same spot in the flow area. That could mean that they are not experiencing enough growth and progress. This is another reason to make conversations about flow a regular occurrence. In the end this can become a management model that provides you with a much better view on how employees feel in their work and what you can do to support them in their development[65].

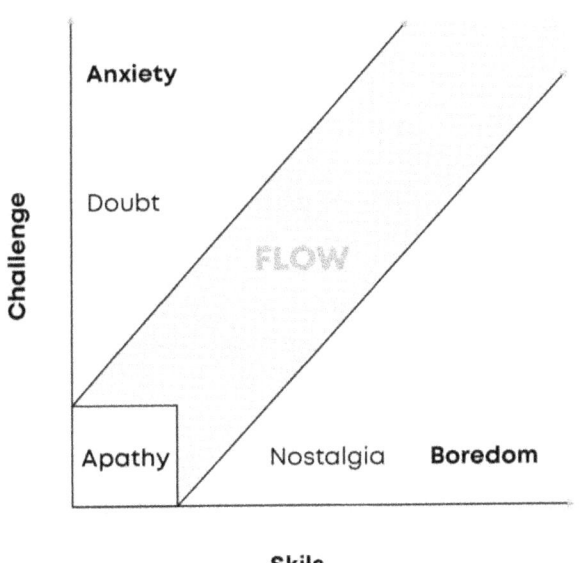

---

65 'An Interview with Cynthia Maxwell' (n.d.), Gelukkigwerken.nl. https://gelukkigwerken.nl/wp-content/uploads/2019/03/An-Interview-with-Cythia-MaxwellV02.pdf. Consulted on May 12, 2020.

Exercise: Having Flow Conversations

How do you have a conversation based on Maxwell's flow graph? It is helpful to draw the flow graph on a piece of paper and to ask employees to mark where they are on the balance of skill and challenge.

Ask the following questions when doing this:
- Where are you now in this model?
- What would you like to change?
- What do you need to move up further in the flow path?

Have these conversations on a regular basis (at least once a month but preferably more often), so that you have a good view on how people feel in their work.

Seven Ideas to Make Progress Visible

1. Choose (set) times with your team where you reflect on the achieved results and successes. For instance, make time during the team meeting to share successes. Try to do this at the beginning of the meeting, because this will influence the atmosphere for the rest of the meeting).

2. Create a WOW-wall. Stick a long strip of paper on a wall and draw a timeline on it. Let everybody stick post-its on this timeline of WOW-moments that they have experienced.

3. Come up with ideas together with your team. What can you do to give more attention to the results that you achieve and make them a set part of the work process itself, so these actions

become set habits?

4. Visualize your workflows using a Kanban board. For instance, draw three fields on a whiteboard: 'To do', 'Doing' and 'Done'. Use colored post-its to show where the projects, activities, and actions are in the process.

5. Give people responsibility to solve problems with a 'problem-solution' wall. When someone experiences a problem, they gather allies and together they come up with possible solutions. The problem and the possible solutions are posted on the wall. Based on that information, management can decide whether money, time, and means are allocated to address the problem. Both the allocation and the rejection will be explained and clearly communicated. When it is a 'yes', the employees will receive the necessary means to get to work on it themselves.

6. Organize a problem grab-bag. Everybody writes down something that irks them on a piece of paper. This piece of paper is folded and thrown into the grab-bag. Divide the team into groups and have every group grab a few problems from the bag and brainstorm about ideas and solutions.

7. Too many bothersome rules or procedures? Organize a 'purple crocodile conference'. A Purple Crocodile is a metaphor for a rule or procedure that gets in the way of progress and happiness at work for employees. All team members name as many purple crocodiles as possible to make a list. Together participants come up with alternatives to the rules.

CONTRIBUTING TO POSITIVITY – FUN

At the Parktheater in Eindhoven in the Netherlands, happiness at work is embedded deeply into the DNA of the organization. From the beginning, Marjon Ouwens-Reus has been involved in putting happiness at work on the map and normalizing it inside the organization. She refers to herself as a Happiness Spreader, because, "Happiness is about spreading positivity." As a manager, your responsibility first and foremost is setting a good example. It helps to exude honest enthusiasm and optimism, but you should never pretend. It is easier if you are a happy and positive person by nature. But even if you are not, you can ensure positivity by taking measures to address your own happiness at work and doing more things that make you happy and to share that.

As a manager you can contribute to the 'positivity' pillar in different ways:

1. Set the right example but beware of superficialities;
2. Put wellbeing on the agenda and make stress a topic of conversations;
3. Make work more fun;
4. Employ ambassadors to spread happiness at work.

Setting the right example

As we have said many times, as a manager your influence on the atmosphere in your team is significant. By being aware of your influence and doing positive things, like Marjon Ouwens-Reus, you can contribute to increasing everybody's positive emotions at work. For the most part this is easier to do than we think. It is mostly about doing small things that are personal, unexpected, and surprising. The effect of these small actions on your team's happiness at work is huge. When you create this environment make sure that it does not become a superficial trick. Things like ping pong tables, free lunches, and the coolest new office setup don't create lasting happiness at work. Small changes and surprises contribute nothing if they are insincere, or if they are being deployed to fudge over or compensate for systemic issues that remain. If you find it hard to take the lead in this as a manager, then look for someone in your team who is better suited for this role. Ultimately, the intention should be that others will follow the positive example. Always make sure that what is done is real and true, and that the team likes it. If you get this wrong don't worry, continue to experiment and try something else.

Putting wellbeing on the agenda

When we look at wellbeing and stress, there are two jobs for you as a manager. The first is to help the employees who are overwhelmed by getting them to slow down. For someone who is stuck in the acceleration trap [Jochen Menges], the brake is often hard to find when someone is on the road to burnout. As a leader or a manager, prioritizing the workload for employees so they know what work is the most important and what work they can say no to is the first step to helping them set healthy boundaries with their work. Overwhelmed employees often lose perspective on how things are going and may therefore think: my work is almost done, if I just hold on a little longer. Intervention is the only way to prevent more damage, and you must call in the help of an expert to ensure a good recovery. Your second responsibility is prevention. Enter into discussion with the members of your team about their energy balance, workload, and stress level, addressing the difference between stress that contributes to top performances and unhealthy (chronic) stress. Discuss with each other how to recognize the different forms of stress. It helps to ask the question: "What does the most stressed version of yourself look like?" That way, team members can learn to recognize for themselves—and their team members—when someone is on the verge of being overwhelmed.

Making work more fun

By dividing the tasks as a team based on the preferences of the people and using their strengths, you can increase joy at work for the entire team. This is also called 'job crafting'. Let your employees shape their job in a way that resembles their ideal job. Often this process takes small tweaks in the responsibilities. IT service provider Nétive does this by supporting people to do what they like to do alongside their job, such as making movies, hosting webinars, and giving workshops. At Parktheater Eindhoven they took it a step further: Managers and employees looked at how they could deploy everyone's talents for the organization. One of the success stories is of an employee who normally sells tickets expanding into making bags from old theater cloth. The profits of those sales are part of an innovation fund that was set up by Parktheater to help new theater employees to develop themselves. Because of the discussions within the entire organization, more room was created for meaningful work. Job crafting has resulted in only 60% of the work of the employees being related to the theater. A whopping 40% of their time is spent on social projects. Another example is an organization where a team wrote all the work that needed to be done on post-its and stuck them on a large planning board. Then all team members could take those jobs they liked to do off the board. This way, job crafting became a team matter that also strengthened collaboration and allowed people to work to their strengths.

Using ambassadors

When you work with a team there are always people who are more enthusiastic than others, colleagues who take more initiative get more energy from the subject of happiness at work than others. Think of it as a pot with popcorn[66]: When you put corn kernels in a pot with a little oil and apply heat, then some of the corn will pop almost immediately. It never happens at the same time for all kernels—there are always a few corn kernels that pop right away and the rest follow later. There are also always a few kernels that do not pop at all. That is just fine; not everybody needs to actively jump in right away. Building a positive work culture is a process, and it works best if people who are excited about it take the lead. Those are your ambassadors, and they help to inspire others and to further fan the flames. Just make sure that the ambassadors don't start regarding it as their responsibility to increase happiness at work for the team.

They are not a new party committee, they are not responsible for making their colleagues happy or to get them to participate and feel involved. However, ambassadors can play a big role in keeping the subject alive and continuing to make it practical.

---

66   Statement of Woohoo Inc.

Seven Ideas for More Positivity in Your Team

1. Name 'fun' and 'positivity' as core values of your team and link behavior to it.

2. Celebrate everything you can celebrate. Make a list together with your team of moments that you can celebrate.

3. Start every meeting with something positive.

4. Install a disco ball with a button that everybody can use. When someone has something to celebrate, they can push the button and the ball will turn. That is the sign that all colleagues, without asking why, get up and applaud. Then afterwards ask what is being celebrated. Make it a conversation to celebrate the wins small or big[67].

5. Moving is healthy and has a favorable effect on your emotions. Take a walk during one-to-one conversations. Consider having your meeting, while standing up instead of sitting around a table. You can be certain they will finish quicker.

6. Participate in a movement challenge or organize one yourself. The toughest one we've heard of? Do planks during your next team meeting (this also ensures quick and efficient meetings).

7. Make having fun a team norm by instituting crazy habits. You will find more ideas in the appendix.

---

67 Example of Tony's Chocolonely.

FROM TEAM LEVEL TO ORGANIZATIONAL LEVEL

When creating a positive team culture, you can mold your role as manager with the help of the pillars of happiness at work. In the previous two chapters you charted this step by step. You now know how to get to work with your team, where you can give space, and how you can contribute through each pillar. The next step is to just do it. Take what suits you and your team from the theory—the examples, the tips, and the exercises—and start experimenting. Then monitor what does and does not work. Where you find something that doesn't suit your team, make adjustments as needed and build on what experiments do go well. And who knows, maybe you'll inspire other teams to get to work on happiness at work too.

Having focused on your individual contribution to happiness at work and a positive work culture—and your role in this as a manager or leader—we will use the next two chapters to zoom out. In this last part of the book we will focus on what an organization can do to integrate happiness at work in operational management. It may be unsurprising to you that a lot can be done at this level.

CHAPTER 11

BUILDING A POSITIVE ORGANIZATIONAL CULTURE

It is Tuesday morning, just a few minutes past ten o'clock. At Guidion, a company that helps clients with technical services in and around the home, music sounds on all floors. Employees leave their computers and gather in the work kitchen. It is time for their daily morning ritual, the Daily Stand Up. At exactly ten past ten a young man in his twenties, wearing a jacket, jeans, and sneakers, climbs on a soapbox and announces that there are 'new faces'. He then asks the newcomers to come forward and to introduce themselves. In less than a minute, three people have introduced themselves. He then invites a colleague to share something about a new project that is in the works. At the end of the standup, the young man steps on the soapbox again and calls out to the kitchen: "What's for lunch today?" A reply comes from someone in the kitchen: "Magda's omelets!" Standing ovation. And then it's over. Everybody returns to their desks.

This 'holy' ritual for Guidion takes place every day in less than ten minutes, always at the same time. It is an important pillar of their organizational culture, where entrepreneurship and happiness at work are central to their workplace culture. Once, when they had to leave the building for a fire drill, they simply held the Daily outside, on the street.

ZOOMING IN ON THE TERM 'ORGANIZATIONAL CULTURE'

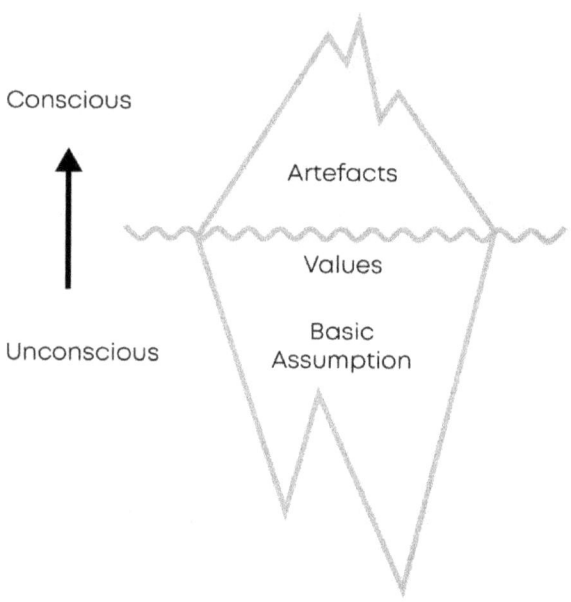

An organization's culture is abstract, and something that people in organizations often find hard to describe clearly. This clarity and understanding is exactly what is necessary to be able to build an organizational culture where people can flourish. To make the term 'culture' more tangible and to truly learn to understand it, management professor Edgar Schein's[68] Culture Iceberg offers a solution.

Schein distinguishes three layers in an organizational culture:

---

68   Schein, Edgar (1999). The Corporate Culture Survival Guide: Sense and Nonsense About Culture Change - Jossey Bass Inc. a John Wiley & Sons, Inc Company

1. **Visible characteristics.** The top layer is the artifacts, or visible elements. This is what you see, hear, and feel when you walk around the office. Think about the interior design and how the office space is used, the language that the employees use, the way people interact and how they address each other, what type of clothing people wear, and the stories that are being told. In short, all the things you can only find by observation. This gives you an immediate impression of how a company operates. Mind you, this is about observation, not interpretation. A closed door, for instance, can mean different things from 'don't come in, I don't want to be disturbed', to 'I am deep in concentration and working in flow is appreciated here'. In this layer you do not interpret, you just observe. The door is closed.

2. **Values and norms.** The second layer that Schein outlines is about the meaning of what you observe. When you talk to people, you discover what your observations mean; what the values, norms, and code of conduct are. What is considered to be right or wrong in an organization, and what is or is not important? Some of those values, norms, and codes of conduct have been defined in documents outlining the organization's vision, mission, and policy. Others are unwritten, but they can be discovered easily because everybody knows them, without speaking about it. A good way to clarify organizational values, norms, and codes of conduct is by asking about the actions you have observed. Such as: "I notice that there are many closed doors here, what does that mean?" Or: "I don't see anyone wearing a suit here; what does that say about how you interact with one another?"

3. **Basic assumptions.** The bottom of the Iceberg—the deepest and least visible layer of an organizational culture—is that of the basic assumptions. They are the convictions, perceptions, and thoughts held by people in the organization. These are often deeply rooted and so obvious to those in the organization that nobody is aware of them. That often makes them difficult to recognize, especially from the inside out. The basic

assumptions that are shared within an organization often form the essence of the culture. They derive from the history and the development of the organization. They are the result of the foundation, growth, success, changes and turning points in the life of the organization; the joint learning process. That is why it is very important to clearly understand those basic assumptions in order to build and influence the culture. The actual changing process starts with becoming aware of it.

> ### Exercise: What About Your Organizational Culture?
>
> The culture iceberg model from Schein can help you understand your own organizational culture better in a number of steps.
>
> Step 1. Look for artifacts
>
> Make a list of the visible elements in your organization. Think about everything you see, hear, and feel when you walk around: the division of departments, the interior of the workplaces, the entry, clothing, how people address each other, notable use of language, behavior in meetings, lunch rituals, etc. Approach this exercise as if you are an outsider and only describe what you observe. Look at things such as behavior during lunchtime, meetings and gatherings, communication channels such as email traffic, the intranet, and the employees' handbook. Ask colleagues to do this too—especially new colleagues—and share your findings. A tip: take a look at other organizations too. What is different there? What stands out? What are the differences? What is specific to your organization?
>
> Step 2. Analyze values, norms, and code of conduct
>
> After you have made a list with visible elements, choose three of the most prominent to analyze further, using the following questions:

- What are our values, norms, and code of conduct, written and unwritten?
- How do these tie in with the visible elements?
- What could be the meaning of each of these observations?
- What does this say about how we think about right and wrong, and about what is important and what is not?

It is helpful to answer these questions for yourself first and then discuss them with colleagues.

Step 3. Dig into the basic assumptions

From the values, norms, and code of conduct you can dig deeper to the basic assumptions of your organization. Start with one or two values and (unwritten) codes of conduct and find out where they come from. Consider the history of the organization and the crucial moments. Who—or what—was involved in creating it? What was a deciding factor? Discuss this with your colleagues. This helps you give you a clearer picture of how the organization developed and how this journey affected the collective behavior.

DEVELOPING AN ORGANIZATION CULTURE

Developing an organizational culture is easier said than done. In real life it is often a long process that does not always have the desired outcome. It takes both time and energy to make it successful. However... it can be done, by taking small intentional steps, trying things out to see what does or does not work, and by continuing to build on what works well. In this process, the so-called Culture Agents play an important role. These can be experts in happiness at work, managers, members of the board, Chief Happiness Officers, or People and Culture Officers, who start building a positive organizational culture from the perspective of the organization.

Culture forms itself

When you want to build a positive culture as a Culture Agent, you need to understand that, in an existing organization, you never start with a blank slate. That is because organizational culture always exists. It starts to emerge as soon as the organization is founded, whether it is consciously built or not. That is because organizations are not tightly regulated systems, they are not the sum of structures, functions, and processes. A culture forms automatically because organizations are living communities in which different realities, individual interests, and human behavior meet. If you don't steer and give direction and meaning to the culture, undesired and ineffective behavior may arise. However, if you are successful in getting a grip on the culture and in creating common starting points, that then leads to collective desired behavior and improves collaboration and performance. Ultimately, a 'positive organizational culture' is not a goal but a means to realize the vision, mission, and organizational goals.

The four steps to change culture

When we work together with our clients, we use four steps to change culture. These seem clear enough on paper—in real life they are less black and white and often merge into one another. It's a matter of setting goals and experimenting. The four steps are:

Step 1. Develop a common language;

Step 2. Map out the organization;

Step 3. Formulate purpose, core values, and desired behavior;

Step 4. Get to work with the Culture Change Wheel.

In this chapter we discuss the first two steps where you prepare for the actual change process. These steps are the basis, and extremely important for successful change—so make sure you take enough time to do this right. The actual change process takes place in steps three and four, which will be discussed in the next chapter.

> **Also Applicable for Teams and Departments**
>
> The four steps to cultural change are not applicable only at an organizational level; they can also be used for building, developing, and maintaining the cultures of teams and departments. The advantage of starting in smaller groups is that you can try out things on a smaller scale first, and then scale up if it works.

STEP 1. DEVELOP A COMMON LANGUAGE

It doesn't matter if your focus is on cultural change or strengthening the existing culture—either way, your first step is always to get people on board. Without the involvement of others in your organization, change is not going to work. Therefore, you need to explain clearly why change is necessary—and you can only get the involvement of your people if you speak the same language. So, if you want to build a positive organizational culture, those involved need to know what your culture is, what happiness at work is—including why it is important and who is responsible for it—and the behavior that contributes to a positive work culture.

Developing a common language means learning together, having discussions, and giving meaning to the goal you wish to reach. Those involved also need the correct tools and skills to change. As Culture Agents you support them by organizing Culture meetings and giving presentations and inspiration. Storytelling is a good aid for this.

> **Storytelling in a Change Process**
>
> The director of an organization wanted to make sure that the 'why' of a cultural change would be ingrained with all his employees. In an earlier phase, he had experienced the power of story-

telling. He asked us if we could start a comparable process to share the new vision of the future with the entire organization. People needed to understand what was coming their way; they had to approach their work in a different manner and adjust their behavior to the new way of thinking. Many employees had become weary and unhappy because of all the changes that had taken place over the years. They needed to feel joy at work again, show their craftsmanship and start working together again. The director wanted to lead them in this and set a good example. He was very aware that how he announced this change would determine whether people would want to join or not. We worked together with him to reserve a prominent spot in his presentation for personal stories—narratives that made his vision for the future very personal and also very clear. The preparation took a couple of days, but it worked out as planned. After his presentation he called us: "It was a success; people were really touched!" That is what stories do: they evoke emotions, connect, and create moments of happiness.

The power of stories

Since prehistoric times people have been communicating with stories. We can remember facts far more easily when told as a story. In our work we receive an enormous amount of information. To ensure that the message you want to convey does not get lost in the avalanche of communication, you would do well to present it as a story. By attaching experiences and emotions to your information, the brain of the listener is more able to process and retain it. When listening to a story we produce oxytocin, the hormone that connects us with others. That makes it easier for us to convert the ideas of someone else's story into our own ideas and experiences. This is referred to as 'neurological linking'. Another reason why we retain information better via stories is that when we process dry facts only two parts of our brain are active, while a well-told story activates many more parts of the brain[69].

> **Annie**: *"Is storytelling a talent or can anybody become a good storyteller?"*

Everybody can tell a story. It is in our nature; we are raised with it. It is possible that you don't do it enough in your adult life and that you have to practice more. A first step is understanding how a story is built. You can learn a lot by observing other storytellers. Every movie, fairy tale, book, catchy TED Talk, and clever anecdote has a certain set of characteristics. Try to analyze the stories you find the most engaging. Which are the elements that you recognize? Who is the main character, what is their goal, and what do they need to conquer? How do they manage to do that in the end, and who or what helps them?

Characteristics of a good story

A good story[70]:

1. is *believable*. Not every detail needs to be literally true, but as a whole, the running thread through it must be true;
2. is built up from a number of set elements. A good story always has a main character, an end goal, and a setback that is conquered (we also call this the turning point, the twist of a story);
3. *connects* people and is repeated again and again. Listeners recognize themselves, add their own experiences and tell the story again;
4. is *human*. Giving an example of a personal challenge, struggle, or something that you have conquered, makes your story believable and authentic;
5. is *visual*. The teller draws a picture in the heads of the

---

69   O'Hara, Carolyn (2014). 'How to Tell a Great Story', Harvard Business Review. https://hbr.org/2014/07/how-to-tell-a-great-story. Consulted on May 15, 2020

70   Schutte, Astrid & Hendriks, Theo (2007). Corporate Stories, Kluwer.

listeners. Speaking in images leads to better understanding. That is because people process images 60 times faster than text[71].

STEP 2. MAP OUT THE ORGANIZATION

Once it is clear what the shared understanding is of happiness at work and a positive work culture in your organization, the current situation must be mapped out. What are the specific characteristics of your organization? How do employees experience the culture? Where do certain actions, habits, and behaviors come from? Which basic assumptions do people share? To what extent do employees experience meaning, transparency, satisfaction, autonomy, connection, psychological safety, and enjoyment in their work? As a Culture Agent, you show what characterizes the organization's culture and how this is experienced by the employees. You do that through observing and speaking with as many people as possible in your organization, by sharing experiences and consulting existing research data. Take a look at what is being said in your employee satisfaction or engagement survey, pay special attention to what is being measured and which questions are asked.

Understanding the organizational culture

To learn to understand the organizational culture, start looking for the shared basic assumptions that shape and color your culture.

Five questions take central stage here[72]:

1. Who are we as an organization?
2. What do we do?
3. Why do we do that? What is our purpose?
4. How do we do what we do?
5. Where and when do we do what we do?

---

71   Boestert, Raymond den & Wolff, Maartje (2017). 'Hoe verhalen bijdragen aan meer werkgeluk', from Vertel! Een boekje open over verhalen vertellen, Vertelacademie Netwerk e.a., Uitgever Vertelacademie.

72   Bremer, Marcella (2018). Developing a Positive Culture Where People and Performance Thrive, Motivational Press.

> **Annie:** "So, basic assumptions are the things that all people in an organization believe? The convictions that everybody in the organization shares about what is supposed to be done, what works, what is right and wrong, and what we should strive for? Can you give me an example?"

The basic assumptions in an organization are the opinions that people share about how things should be done. Take a company like Tony's Chocolonely. The basic assumption here is that slavery is wrong and should be abolished. Of course, there are a lot more people in the world who share this opinion. When you work at Tony's, this opinion leads to something that you work on every day, together with your colleagues. That makes it a basic assumption of the entire organization. When you know—and share—the basic assumptions as a team, department, or organization, you have everyone's combined energy working towards this common goal and you can achieve more. This exponential energy is what makes it so powerful when organizations can communicate their basic assumption(s) clearly.

Basis of culture: back to the source

The more concretely you are able to answer the five questions, the more insight you will become regarding the basis of your culture (the questions in this text box are helpful for this). That is because the basic assumptions arise from the history of the organization, and can often be traced back to persons or groups who were very meaningful for your organization: the founder, a certain director, an inventor, or a group of people who started something special together. Adjustments and changes in the different stages of life of the organization are also important, such as a change that brought your company to the brink of disaster—or one that saved it. Think about mergers, acquisitions, takeovers, or the drastic changing of a production method or way of working. These types of important moments—turning points—can lead to common ideas and convictions about what is important and which behavior is desirable.

> **Questions to Help Find Basic Assumptions**
>
> - Why was our organization founded and for whom? How do we make an impact?
> - Why do we exist and what is our vision, our mission, and our goal(s)?
> - Which persons and/or events were decisive in the history of our organization? What were their ideas, notions, thoughts, con victions, and how did they convert them into strategy, structure, and policy?
> - How do we regard people in our organization? Do we believe that people are good by nature or that they need to be checked on?
> - What do we all think is really important? For instance, are we more focused on results or on relationships, for the short term or on the long term? Is utilizing opportunities and possibilities our way of working, or do we prefer to avoid risks?
> - What were the successes, the failures, and the turning points during the lifetime of the organization?
> - If we had to use four words to describe what our organization is all about, which words would we use?
> - Which stories and anecdotes continue to be retold (for instance during office parties, at the coffee machine, during official occasions)? Which are the stories that you tell to your new starters?

Direct and indirect influencing factors

What can you do to influence the organization's behavior? Based on the theory of Schein[73] There are two influence mechanisms: direct and indirect.

Direct influence: copy, coach, correct

People's behavior in the organization and the daily business are not only the outcome of culture, they also influence the culture directly[74]. That is because culture is shaped through interactions between people: things that are said, people—consciously or unconsciously—copying each other's behavior, and directing and correcting each other when things threaten to go wrong. Think about exemplary behavior of colleagues (copy), the explanation you receive about habits (coach), or the result of jokes when you do something that the group doesn't appreciate (correct[75]). Think about feedback that you receive and give. Think about leadership behavior, the focal points of the top leaders. What do they consider to be important? What is their behavior like when it becomes difficult or even critical? How are status, rewards, and appointments awarded? Which successes are celebrated? And how do processes such as recruitment, and departure of employees work? Reflecting on these areas help you to identify the way the organization behaves, what we really mean, and uncover those underlying assumptions. Does what we do align with what we say?

Indirect influence

Some factors influence how people behave in an organization, but in a roundabout way. These factors contain, among other things, the formulated vision, mission, and values of a company, the design and the structure of the organization, the systems and procedures, formal guidelines, corporate identity, stories, myths, rituals, and design.

---

73   Schein, Edgar, Ibid.
74   Tennekes, Johannes (1996). Organisatiecultuur. Een antropologische visie, Garant Uitgevers.
75   Marcella Bremer, Developing a Positive Culture Where People and Performance Thrive, Motivational Press.

> **Exercise: Directly and Indirectly Influencing Factors**
>
> Which direct and indirect influencing factors do you recognize in your organization, and what are their results? Make a list and discuss them with a colleague. It is more effective if everyone involved makes their own list and then discusses it with each other. Examples of what could be on the list are:
>
> • At our company, hard work is rewarded with compliments and promotions. This leads to people doing overtime more often than is good for them (direct influence).
>
> • When there was a crisis, management made the choice not to fire anybody. This resulted in higher trust in our leaders (direct influence).
>
> • Managers are not open about the mistakes that they make. This results in making it difficult to admit mistakes and means we do not learn enough when we make mistakes (direct influence).
>
> • During our monthly meetings we tell each other anecdotes about how we successfully apply our values. That way we continue to realize what our core values mean and what the suitable behavior is (indirect influence).
>
> • In our organization you can see how important a person is by the size of their office (indirect influence).

THE FOUNDATION HAS BEEN LAID

When you have taken sufficient time for the first two steps in changing culture—creating a common language and mapping out the organization—you have created the right foundation. Taking the time for this ensures that you have a more complete, and therefore better image of where you stand as an organization, where you want to go to, what is needed to get there, and where you can start. A good foundation also helps in creating a broad support base for the changing process that follows. In chapter 12 we will explore steps three and four in changing culture.

CHAPTER 12
THE CULTURE CHANGE WHEEL

Working on your organizational culture is a continuous quest for opportunities to improve the organizational behavior and performance, on an individual, team, and organizational level. This process is not an easy fix. In fact, it is a process that will never be finished. In this chapter we will continue with cultural change steps three and four:

> Step 3. Formulating purpose, core values and desired behavior
> Step 4. Getting to work with the Culture Change Wheel

STEP 3. FORMULATING PURPOSE, CORE VALUES AND DESIRED BEHAVIOR

The outlines for the desired culture are drawn with Culture Change step two, mapping the organization, where you looked into the organization and what contributes to the organizational performance. In Culture Change step three, you make this more concrete by explicitly defining the purpose and the core values of the organization, and translating these to desired behavior. In a positive organizational culture the purpose, values, and the desired behavior correspond with the four P's: purpose, people, progress, and positivity. Of course every organization is different, so the point of focus will differ for every organization too.

Purpose and basic assumptions

Building a positive organizational culture starts with formulating a clear purpose. You don't need to come up with something new and creative, because the purpose of your organization already exists. It is about 'uncovering' your purpose. You probably already found it in your quest for the basic assumptions, because the purpose is closely connected to the most important basic assumption(s) of the organization. They both arise from the origin. In fact, in some organizations—like at Tony's Chocolonely—the most important basic assumption is expressed in the purpose. This step where you put into words what your organization is all about. (The questions in step one of the previous chapter are helpful for this too.)

> ### 🏋 Exercise: Organization Purpose for a Positive Culture
>
> To what extent does the purpose of your organization contribute to a positive organizational culture? It helps to answer the following questions:
>
> 1. Why was the organization founded?
> 2. Which added value is delivered for whom?
> 3. When is the organization successful, with which products, services, and actions?
> 4. How does our purpose contribute to more happiness at work, to the feeling of meaning and progress, connection, and enjoyment?
> 5. What did you discover?
>
> Next, ask to what extent the purpose is ambitious and inspiring and spurs people to action. Questions to ask are:
>
> 1. What do we think that needs to be changed in the world, in the industry or sector in which we operate?
> 2. How can we contribute?
>
> Looking at your answers, the last and maybe most important question is: think about your purpose: what is good and what can be improved?

Annie: *"I'm looking for inspiration. Which organizations have a purpose that contributes to a positive organizational culture?"*

More than ever there are organizations that strive for a positive organizational culture and integrate this in their purpose. Four well-known examples of purposes that contribute to happiness at work and a positive work culture are:

Tony's Chocolonely: *Together we can make the chocolate industry 100% slave free.*

Patagonia: *Build the best product; cause no unnecessary harm, use business to inspire and implement solutions to the environmental crisis.*

Viisi: *We want to make the financial world better, more sustainable, and more focused on the long term. We want to create an environment in which everybody at Viisi realizes his or her dreams, their 'personal why'.*

Dr. Reddy's: *Good Health can't wait. In the pharmaceutical industry we have the unique role and the ethical and moral necessity to maintain patients' health and to make them well again, all over the world.*

They describe what the organization contributes, and for whom. They also contain a challenging ambition and indicate for whom they make a difference and how.

Involve as many people as possible

For some organizations, their purpose is crystal clear. For others, finding it can be a long (and sometimes frustrating) process. We always advise our clients to involve as many people as possible. Often different employees—and other stakeholders—have different pieces of the puzzle. On top of that, the joint quest to what drives the organization contributes to everybody's involvement. It can also be helpful to ask help from an external facilitator who guides the process and asks the right questions. That increases the chances for success too. Again, it is a procedure of formulating, reformulating, and fine tuning. This takes a lot of time, but the moment you find the purpose, it will feel magical. We often hear from our clients that—in hindsight—their purpose was very obvious. In fact, they didn't see it earlier because it was so obvious. This was also the case with Guidion.

> **Purpose of Guidion**
> Guidion was founded more than 12 years ago based around the belief that entrepreneurship makes people flourish. This philosophy is deeply ingrained into the DNA of the organization. So deep, that for the longest time they didn't see that this was where the basis of their purpose lay. In their quest for meaning several 'whys' popped up. For a while they tried to shape their purpose as 'worldwide residential happiness'. But whatever they came up with, they were not successful in making this concrete and practical. It wasn't until they went back to basics and started to discuss the reasons why they were founded in the first place, that it became clear. Today, Guidion's purpose is described as 'Unleashing Entrepreneurship'. At Guidion, everything is about creating an environment in which people can evolve and reach their full potential. This belief is the foundation of the establishment of the organization.

Core values help to make choices

In addition to a clear purpose you also need a set of core values to realize your desired organizational culture. These values clarify what is considered important in the organization, how alternatives are weighed, and how choices are made. When we talk about core values, less is more. Three or four is enough; we discourage five or more, that is too much to remember easily. We look at which values are the most characteristic for the organization, and to what extent they contribute

HAPPINESS AT WORK
THE MOST NATURAL THING IN THE WORLD.
HAPPINESS AT WORK PAYS OFF.
FOR YOURSELF WHEN YOU ARE HAPPY, YOU ARE: HEALTHIER, MORE VITAL, MORE CHEERFUL, MORE SOCIAL AND MORE SUCCESSFUL FOR ORGANISATIONS: HAPPIER EMPLOYEES ARE MORE INVOLVED, MORE PRODUCTIVE, MORE COOPERATIVE, MORE CREATIVE AND MORE INNOVATIVE. THEY ARE LESS LIKELY TO CALL IN SICK AND THERE IS A DECREASED CHANCE THEY WILL EXPERIENCE A BURNOUT. HAPPINESS AT WORK IS ABOUT MEANINGFUL WORK, HEALTHY RELATIONSHIPS, DEVELOPMENT AND HAVING **FUN** AND ABOUT STOPPING UNNECESSARY RULES, POWER, COMPLICATED PROCESSES AND PROCEDURES, ABSENTEEISM UNMOTIVATED COLLEAGUES AND TERRIBLE MANAGERS. LET'S CREATE A WORKPLACE TO STIMULATE FUN, APPRECIATION POSITIVE FEEDBACK, AWESOME CHALLENGES, TRUST, MEANINGFUL RESULTS AND OWN RESPONSIBILITIES LET US, AS EMPLOYEES, EMPLOYERS ENTREPRENEURS, ORGANISATIONS AND ESPECIALLY AS **HUMAN BEINGS WORK** TOGETHER TO MAKE HAPPINESS AT WORK THE MOST NATURAL THING IN THE WORLD.

Together we can make a difference. Are you in?

Sign the manifesto on
www.internationalweekofhappinessatwork.com

to happiness at work and the success of the organization. Of course, this is not something that is up to us as consultants to decide. We ask as many people as possible—where practical—to participate in the conversation. In the end, we formulate together the corresponding behavior into a maximum of ten 'behavior rules'. Without those explicit starting points employees give their own meaning to the values, and may end up with a very differentiated set of explanations—possibly mismatched with your intentions. By drawing up concrete, communal starting points, together you can build your culture in a more targeted way.

As mentioned previously, to maintain a positive organizational culture it is important that the core values correspond with the four pillars of happiness at work: 'purpose', 'people', 'progress' and 'positivity'. For instance, the values of Tony's Chocolonely are 'critical' (related to their purpose), 'entrepreneurial' (linked to progress), 'quirky' (fits with people), and 'to make you happy' (positivity). Happiness at work is also important for Guidion, whose core values are in line with the four P's.

> **Core Values of Guidion**
>
> Guidion has formulated its core values as: 'Can-do-is-you' (in line with their purpose), 'Share the Fun' (positivity), 'Let's grow' (progress) and 'Happy to help' (people). These values have not been thought up by a management team or external agency; the employees have formulated them together. Once defined, these values were dressed up in a catchy phrase and translated to behavioral principles. That way they are tangible and become leading principles for everything that everybody does in the organization. The first thing you see when you step out of the elevator at Guidion are the core values painted on the wall. You will also see them in other locations in the building. They are being brought up in every Daily and during every meeting. The result is, that at Guidion—contrary to many other organizations—everybody recites the values effortlessly and knows exactly what they mean. You recognize this in everybody's behavior.

Create a manifesto?

A clear purpose (why) and explicit values (how) must ultimately be translated into appropriate behavioral principles. How do we behave ourselves here and what do we do or not do? You can put purpose, values, and behavioral principles on paper in a manifesto. This is an abbreviated rendering of the starting positions of an organization, department, or team with the goal of giving people space to make their own choices, within the mutually agreed upon principles.

> **Cultural Bricks of Independer**
>
> At Independer they formulated core values and made them into 'cultural bricks'. They have placed these on the floor at the entrance of their building. This way everybody who comes to visit can see what Independer stands for. That also contributes to the happiness at work of their employees.

Pitfalls and solutions

Even though finding your purpose and core values is a beautiful process, there are also some pitfalls. The first is that you can get stuck in the formulation. We often see culture agents who get to work with formulating the purpose but get stuck in looking for the most beautiful phrase that encompasses as much as possible. They often don't dare to choose what they stand for. This can cause the purpose to become meaningless and too general. It is not necessary to include everything (it won't work anyway). What does work is making choices and formulating a clear ambition. The second pitfall is adopting the marketing slogan that works well in client communications as the organizational purpose, without it being recognized by the employees. A purpose must be real and felt by everybody. The third pitfall is that those involved, once purpose and core values have been found, do not take enough time to talk about what the words mean and what the aligned behavior is. We often see 'confusion of tongues' with values, like a well-known organization that had noted 'communication, integrity, respect and excellence' as core values and then went bankrupt a year later after fraud and mismanagement were discovered. Apparently, the word 'integrity' is interpreted differently by different people. The last pitfall is that the purpose and values are communicated and repeated insufficiently. Have them show up in all aspects of the organization and communication: in the design and the interior of the building, during meetings, events, parties, whatever you can think of. The more and the more often, the better.

Behavior in a positive organizational culture

How do people behave in a positive organizational culture? In other words: which behavior principles are leading here? When we look at organizations that perform well because they have a positive organizational culture, we see a number of common behavioral characteristics; these are in line with the pillars of happiness at work:

1. The higher goal, the purpose, the common interest is number one and the work is geared to 'getting the job done'. Employees are not occupied with hierarchy and status.
2. Collegiality takes center stage. People ask each other for help and help each other. They talk about 'we', not 'I'.
3. Employees dare to be vulnerable. They openly discuss their mistakes and take time for self-reflection.
4. In meetings, everybody speaks for a roughly equal amount of time.
5. People don't avoid difficult discussions. They hold these in a constructive way and are open with the giving and receiving of feedback.
6. Employees are given responsibility and take ownership. Seen from the quadrants of ownership[76], they are mostly in the quadrant in the top right-hand corner—that of the leader.
7. Employees have a growth mindset. They actively search for possibilities to learn, to grow and to develop themselves. They react positively to new challenges.
8. People assume the good in others and use positive language.

---

76   Diamond, Dan (2015). Beyond Resilience: Trench-Tested Tools to Thrive Under Pressure, NoggingStorm.

9. Employees don't talk about each other, but with each other. They don't (or rarely) engage in 'drama behavior' such as complaining, nagging, venting and judging.
10. People are sincerely curious about the opinion of others and therefore ask many questions, about as much as they offer their opinion.

STEP 4. GETTING TO WORK WITH THE CULTURAL CHANGE WHEEL

Coming up with a desired culture and putting it on paper is relatively simple. It is much harder to make sure that this culture reaches the capillaries of the organization and becomes reality. This is where the real work starts.

Changing organizational culture is not a linear and structured process. To bring structure and to coordinate the different interventions, we use the Cultural Change Wheel[77]. This is an uncluttered, practically applicable model that fits well with what Schein explains about directly and indirectly influencing factors.

In the center of the model, the axis of the wheel, you find the purpose, core values, and behavioral principles. For a positive organizational structure, you have formulated those based on the four pillars of happiness at work (purpose, people, progress, and positivity). The purpose, core values and behavioral principles form the starting point of your vision; that must be in line with how the organization functions, and what must change. Then you have three elements, the so-called Cultural Elements (based on Schein's influencing factors), that you can deploy to shape the actual changing process.

---

77 Daimler, Melissa (2018). 'Why Great Employees Leave "Great Cultures"', Harvard Business Review. https://hbr.org/2018/05/why-great-employees-leave-great-cultures. Consulted on January 3, 2020.

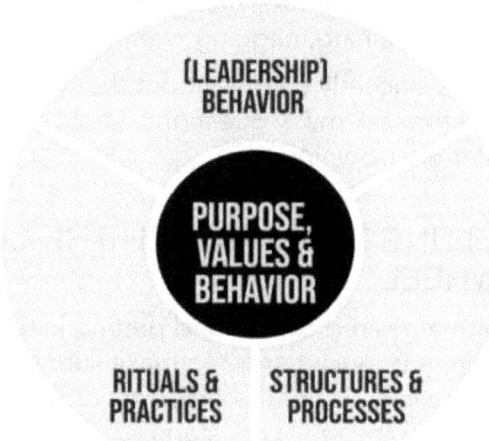

Those three cultural elements are:

- **A.** leadership and exemplary behavior;
- **B.** structures, systems and processes;
- **C.** rituals, habits, and customs.

Cultural gaps

The three cultural elements help you to realize the desired organizational culture step by step. The most important is that the cultural elements and the starting point (purpose, core values, and desired behavior) are aligned with each other. Do the leaders of the organization show the desired behavior? Are processes and structures devised in a way that they promote the desired behavior or at least don't block them? And do the customs and rituals emphasize what is truly important for the organization? Is the communication directed to convey purpose, values, and desired behavior? Is the message aligned with day-to-day reality? Because no matter what beautiful ideas, concepts, plans, and stories you may have, if they are not underlined by the visible behavior, they are of no use. If you send two different messages, people will believe what they see and experience rather than what is being said. In the organizations that we work with, we see painful examples of how leadership, structures, processes, rituals, and customs contradict the desired organizational culture.

As an example, we had a client who named healthy work-life balance one of their core values, because structurally there were way too many long workdays, causing the number of mistakes to increase. To change this, behavioral principles were drafted and communicated to the different teams. So far, so good. It just turned out that in real life the way in which the targets were set up created the need to work overtime. Supervisors who made extra hours in order to achieve the targets received explicit appreciation for that. You can see the mismatch here: there was a difference between the core value 'healthy work-life balance' on one side, and goal setting and exemplary behavior of supervisors on the other side. When we brought that up, they suddenly became aware that they did not adhere to this core value themselves. These types of differences between what you say—your purpose and your core values—and what really happens, is what we call cultural gaps.

> DOING WHAT YOU SAY
> AND
> SAYING WHAT YOU DO,
> THAT'S WHAT IT'S ALL
> ABOUT.

These cultural gaps can appear everywhere on the Cultural

Change Wheel: between purpose/values and (leadership) behavior, between purpose/values and processes, between purpose/values and rituals, and between the cultural elements themselves. Seeing the cultural gaps (monitoring), understanding where they come from (analyzing) and solving them is key when building and maintaining a positive organizational culture. We will discuss each of the parts.

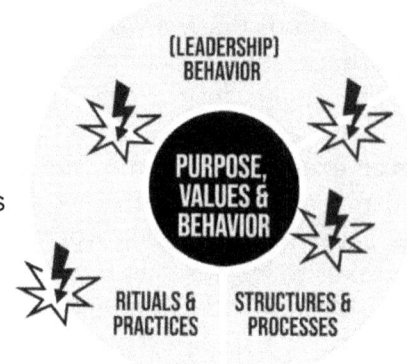

Exemplary and leadership behavior

Putting desired behavior into practice starts at the top. Leaders should be the first to set a good example. Only then will employees take it seriously. In many cases it is necessary to coach leaders on this; it is very difficult to look at your own behavior with a clear view. A fresh pair of eyes puts things into perspective. It also helps when leaders and supervisors encourage the desired behavior when coaching employees. If you want people to take ownership and responsibility for their results, then as a supervisor you must create the space for employees to do that. Or if your values state that people always come first, then you cannot just fire people when financial results are not as expected. Southwest Airlines understands that very well. When all air traffic in the United States was stopped after 9/11/2001, the supervisors told their people: "There are no flights, we have no work. But we will not fire anybody. Go do something else temporarily, as soon as we can fly again, we will call you." Living up to their own values contributes to the positive organizational culture of Southwest Airlines, and that showed in the results. It is the only airline that was in the red for just one quarter after September 11, before quickly returning to profit[78].

---

78   Glynn, Matt (2014). 'Ex-Southwest Airlines ceo offers lessons in leadership from post-9/11 crisis', The Buffalo News. https://buffalonews.com/2014/05/19/ex-southwest-airlines-ceo-offers-lessons-in-leadership-from-post-911-crisis. Consulted

> **Exemplary Behavior at Dr. Reddy's**
>
> Another example of a successful cultural change where exemplary behavior played an important role comes from Dr. Reddy's Pharma. Pharma's rapid international growth had caused the organization to drift away from their purpose and values. Top management decided to reformulate the organization, taking a year for the process and involving as many stakeholders as possible. After that year they described their purpose in four words: 'Good health can't wait.' Instead of communicating this directly—internally and externally—they decided to first adjust their own behavior. They searched for examples within the organization where the desired behavior was already shown, and started telling those stories with the goal of starting a movement. At the same time, step-by-step processes were aligned to the new mission. As soon as the desired behavior was applied on a large scale, they asked everybody internal to the organization to make an official commitment to it by signing a manifesto. Only then did they start communicating their new purpose statement externally. The changing process was shaped by just doing it, by setting the right example themselves and by letting people join in[79].

An Example for Others

To be an example for others it helps to look at yourself critically. Do your actions correspond with

---

on May 13, 2020.
79   Walker, Bryan & Soule, Sarah A. (2017). 'Changing Company Culture Requires a Movement, Not a Mandate', Harvard Business Review. https://hbr.org/2017/06/changing-company-culture-requires-a-movement-not-a-mandate. Consulted on December 12, 2019.

what you say and what you would like to project? Many people have a blind spot for their own behavior, especially where it concerns ingrained patterns and subconscious basic assumptions. If you are serious about working on that, investigate what your convictions are and ask for feedback. Your blind spots become more visible when you take a different perspective, and that is an important step for change. You can only learn or unlearn behavior once you have gained a fuller understanding of what you overlook in yourself.

To design your desired behavior, you can use the change checklist from chapter 7:
- Step 1: take a look at your motivation.
- Step 2: investigate your abilities.
- Step 3: make sure that the environment supports the correct behavior.

Which behavior do you stimulate?

Giving the right example is one way to stimulate desired behavior. Another way is to 'reward' the correct behavior—explicitly or implicitly. For instance, who has the best chance for a promotion at your company—those who collaborate best with colleagues and let others shine, or the people who stand on stage and receive the applause? With these choices, you implicitly indicate which behavior is preferred and which is frowned upon. People believe what they see happening rather than what is being said.

Systems and processes

Management structures, reward systems, feedback, and communication processes: an organization has many formal and informal processes and structures. Some have a direct influence on the culture, such as assessment and reward systems, others are more indirect, such as the organization structure and strategic processes. Ideally, to ensure that the desired behavior reaches the entire organization, you should scrutinize all systems, structures, and processes and ask yourself why they are the way they are. To which behavior do they lead? To what extent is that desirable—and if it is not, how can we (re)design the systems and processes so that they do contribute? Addressing everything at once is not the solution. Taking it step by step is less cluttered and therefore works better. Continuous improvement is key in this process. Just start somewhere, for instance with a process that needs to be adjusted anyway or with a structure that is the cause of much dissatisfaction. If you really don't know where to start, we can give you some ideas.

Replace the term 'human resource management'

We consider that the first step to building a positive work culture is to replace the term 'Human Resource Management'. With this terminology, people are regarded as a resource—an object to be used—and even though it may not be your intention, in real life that often leads to mainly looking at the output of an employee. We often have discussions about this with clients and colleagues. "What difference does a name make?" is an objection we often hear. We don't agree with such a sentiment. Language plays an important role in building and maintaining your organizational culture. It decides how you regard your colleagues, what your direction is, and which goals, tasks, and responsibilities belong to the department of Human Resource Management.

If you don't want to regard people as mere resources, that must become clear from the way you talk about them. Which alternative names could you come up with? There are plenty of good examples. Organizations such as Guidion, Tony's Chocolonely and Independer use names like People & Culture, Culture and Colleague or People First. When you change the name of a department, often something else happens too: the focus of the department shifts. For a department named 'Culture and Colleague' it is very logical to not only deal with salaries and work benefits, but also to build a positive organizational culture.

Other systems, structures, and processes that you can address for a positive work culture are, among others:

    1. hiring policy;

2. reward systems;
3. assessment systems (and development);
4. communication processes.

Hiring policy

The behavior of employees is the strongest influence on organizational culture, which makes the hiring and onboarding policy very important. Hiring the 'wrong' people or not making it clear what the desired behavior is during the onboarding process will have a huge influence on collaboration and performance. In fact, one bad apple can completely spoil the atmosphere within a team. That's why the policy of the food chain Pret-a-Manger is 'Hire for attitude, train for skills'. They say: 'We can teach everyone how to make a sandwich, but not how they can be happy.' Organizations that place importance on positive organizational culture make their attitude and behavior a focal point of their hiring policy. Guidion, for instance, checks on how candidates score on organizational values during recruitment and selection. Their questionnaire is mainly about motivation and drivers. That list also forms the basis for the assessment during the selection procedure. The goal is to make abstract things—such as values—concrete and to 'objectively' test people on that. Southwest Airlines values respect more than the best certification. In one instance, a pilot with an impressive resumé applied for a job during a period where the airline was in dire need of good pilots[80]. However, the man also had a gigantic ego. When he reported at the desk for his application interview he behaved arrogantly and rudely towards the receptionist, who passed this observation on to the recruiter. When the recruiter came downstairs, he shook hands with the applicant and thanked him for coming. "You really have an impressive resumé, however this is the end of the procedure. For us, respect and good manners are just as important as knowledge and skills." Southwest Airlines is right: no matter how good someone looks on paper, if they don't fit in the organization or in the team, it ultimately won't work out.

---

80   Sutton, Robert I. (2010). The No Asshole Rule: Building a Civilized Workplace and Surviving One That Isn't, Little, Brown.

> **Tony's Chocolonely: Color to the Culture**
>
> At Tony's Chocolonely, applicants get the question: "What really makes you happy?" They also explicitly ask for extraordinary, weird, or notable hobbies or characteristics. The idea behind this is that everyone within Tony's has a story and is unique in their own way. That doesn't just color the organization culture, it also fits their core values 'willfulness' and 'make you smile'.

Reward systems

As we said before, salary and work benefits do not immediately contribute to more happiness at work; they mostly influence job satisfaction. Therefore, it is especially important that a reward policy does not stand in the way of someone's happiness at work. The way in which people are rewarded directly influences their behavior. Think about performance rewards based on individual bonuses, for instance, which often lead to mutual competition and block good collaboration. When you as an organization put your people first with the intention of enabling them to flourish, they must first feel safe. Trying out things, making mistakes, and asking questions—these do not happen if you ultimately 'have to pay for it'. The same reward model for all employees—completely independent of performance—contributes to psychological safety. Mortgage Consultant Viisi has such a policy.

> **The Reward Policy of Viisi**
>
> Mortgage Consultant Viisi is a growing organization with approximately 40 employees. They work according to the Holacracy principle. In their quest for a suitable salary model, they explored all kinds of systems, eventually concluding that salary structures at many financial institutions are unnecessarily opaque and complex. To address this, Viisi developed a model that is simple enough that it

> fits on a single piece of paper. They use five areas of expertise, where everybody ends up in one of these areas and is scaled based on the number of years of specific work experience. Every year on their 'work anniversary'—the day that they are hired—they receive a salary raise that is the same for everybody in the relevant area of expertise. The size of that annual raise depends on market rates. Viisi first determined that they wanted to offer rewards in the top quartile and then asked employees to ask previous colleagues and other peers what they earn. Based on the different data points they drew a growth line and calculated the yearly increase. This way the salary is honest, transparent, and not linked to the daily work or everyone's performance[81].

Assessment systems

Assessment systems also have a big influence on behavior[82]. At the same time, employees often have a negative view or experience of the yearly performance review process. In many organizations, performance reviews are held once or twice a year to discuss what went wrong or could be done better. However, these types of yearly conversations don't contribute to better performance. In fact, they are demotivating. How can you summarize someone's activity for an entire year in only one conversation? That doesn't enhance development and growth.

> **Annie:** *"It sounds like performance reviews are not really meaningful for employees. Then why do we do it? Are they useful for managers?"*

> *The current approach of yearly performance reviews is not only demotivating for employees; supervisors are*

---

81   Moedt, Kristel & Luiting, Eveliese (2020). 'Transparant belonen, met Marc-Peter Pijper van Viisi', People masterminds (podcast).
82   Moedt, Kristel & Luiting, Eveliese (2019). 'Stop met performance management, start met talent management, met Kilian Wawoe', People masterminds (podcast).

also not exactly thrilled by them. They often don't like doing them and the whole process takes a lot of time. HR advisor and author Killian Wawoe calculated the time spent and the yield of these yearly performance reviews. Wawoe concluded that managers spend 100–200 hours per year on the assessment process—setting goals, reviewing them, filling out forms, chasing after the results, discussing it with HR, etc. For the Netherlands alone the costs are about a billion Euros per year, at a return of zero. Reason enough to stop doing this and to handle it differently.

The new way of assessing

What would be a good alternative for the yearly performance review? First of all, it is important to have conversations a lot more frequently and to give feedback on the different parts of someone's performance. Acknowledge their contribution at the moment of completion of a project, or look at a certain month or a stage in someone's learning process and give feedback about that. Secondly, it is important to be specific in your advice; practical directions can help people improve. Thirdly, it helps to cut up the conversation in two parts. Currently, performance reviews assess the past period and at the same time look at what to improve in the future: coaching for the future learning process. That is a difficult combination. In practice, the majority of the review is spent on looking back and explaining the assessment. It is in our nature to pay more attention to negative things and to remember those better, so that is what we focus on. That is why people lose motivation and why performance reviews do not promote the learning process. By separating the assessment and the learning process there is more room for growth. You will then have conversations that are about the assessment with your manager, and coaching conversations that are about improvement, perhaps with colleagues in the team. Fourthly, it also helps to detach the reward system from the assessment. That will lead to having conversations with better content about results and development, without it having immediate consequences on income. It is great when you also give people autonomy in determining their learning goals and collecting the 'evidence' for the outcomes. Fifthly and finally, it helps to not just talk about someone's competences and skills, but also about their dreams and ambitions. This gives you a greater insight on how someone sees themselves, what makes them happy, what their talents or motivations are, and which goals they want to reach.

Annie: "What does the role of the coaching colleague in the team look like?"

Coaching within a team is about colleagues helping each other to develop and to grow. This can be done by intervision and reflection. For some professions such as lawyers, physicians, and accountants this is standard procedure—in the Netherlands they are obligated to spend 40 hours every year on professional development. The premise is this: you enter into a discussion with a colleague both as a professional, where neither of you pretends to know better. Before you start, create an agenda based on points that are important for you. Your sparring partner asks questions about it and gives tips on improvement. This way you will end up with very specific points on what you need to do to improve[83].

Good Examples

More and more companies approach their performance reviews with greater flexibility and creativity. Employees of the Parktheater in Eindhoven have developed a game together, based around a conversation between the supervisor and employee on personal development goals the employee has set. A Dutch travel agency uses four questions in their periodical performance reviews:

1. What have you contributed to your personal

---

83   Ibid

targets in the past period?

2. What have you contributed to the organization goals?

3. What have you contributed to the world?

4. What goals do you set for yourself for the next period?

Communication processes

Communication plays a big role in shaping and refining your culture. Open communication also contributes to psychological safety and connection. On one hand, communicating is easy—we do it all day. At the same time, communication is extremely difficult because everybody has their own interpretation of what is being communicated. Therefore, it is not evident that communication is always effective and that initiatives and goals are aligned. An organization has formal communication structures and processes, but a lot more informal ones: among colleagues, within teams, between departments, and at the organizational level. This encompasses a lot of topics: from language use and giving feedback, to sharing strategic information (purpose, goals, results, and successes), and task-oriented information regarding what teams are involved with and how they collaborate. How can you influence these formal and informal processes so that they contribute to a positive organizational culture? The most important lesson you can take from organizations with a positive culture is that the process of building and maintaining the culture has been given a lot of consideration. It has the highest priority and must contribute to maximum transparency. The communication assumes trust, involves as many people as possible, and leads to mutual connection. Good and positive communication is embedded carefully in processes and structures and is shaped in rituals and customs. The communication of organizations like Guidion and Nétive is approached rhythmically. They have set daily, weekly, monthly, quarterly, and yearly meetings.

Rituals and customs

The weekly stand-up, the morning meeting, Friday drinks, and the way in which people hold meetings: there are many habits and customs in organizations. Sometimes the employees do not even realize that they exist. That is a shame, because such moments and occasions are explicitly suitable to draw attention to purpose, values, and the pillars of happiness at work, and to stimulate desired behavior. By making these into meaningful moments—rituals—you build structurally upon a positive organizational culture. Take Guidion's Daily, for instance: this consultation has a strict, repeating format, at a set time and with a set limit (less than ten minutes), set themes, and a fixed structure. The format is directly linked to the core values and the pillars of happiness at work. In this way it helps to direct organizational behavior. One of the core values of Guidion is 'Let's Grow', and in the Daily all employees are invited to get on the soap box and speak in front of the group. Within the guidelines there is a lot of room for autonomy, and everybody is invited to contribute something. Meeting daily builds connections, and the stories that are being told are often about how purpose and core values are put into practice. The approach and the tone of voice of the Daily are always positive. This is a beautiful example of how you can make a meaningful ritual from a practical habit. Other organizations that also consciously build on a positive organizational culture—such as Nétive, Tony's Chocolonely, and Independer—see rituals as important building blocks.

A few examples:

> **Example Rituals**
>
> At Independer they have a monthly 'Long Table', where colleagues cook for each other and have lunch together at one long table. This ritual contributes to their feeling of connectedness.
>
> At Tony's Chocolonely they hold 'critical value sessions', where everybody is invited to speak their mind about a subject that is relevant in the orga-

nization or outside of it. Not only does this help to solidify their core values—'critical' and learning together—but it also ensures that everybody dares to say what's on their mind, thus contributing to psychological safety.

At Nétive they have the Start-Stop-Continue principle where teams decide for themselves which activities to start, stop, or continue. This increases their sense of progress and autonomy.

At Tony's Chocolonely the whole company takes a trip every year and they all take a course together. The goal is to foster more connection, better collaboration, and learning together.

At Guidion they have the Happiness Day, an extra day off that people can take whenever they want and spend the time as they choose, as long as they share their experience with their colleagues in the form of a picture, video, or blog. The idea behind this is that sharing happiness contributes to the happiness of others.

At Tony's Chocolonely they organize a monthly Typical Tony's Time: the onboarding of a whole week with different sessions, including a session on their culture for new employees. The week ends with the Yep-Nope Tony's quiz, to test if the newbies really understand how a 'Tony' should behave.

Nétive holds monthly soapbox sessions where colleagues share special hobbies and interests to get to know each other in a different way.

There are plenty of other fun examples of making happiness at work specific via rituals and customs. In the attachment you will find several ideas for inspiration to shape the organization rituals in your organization.

FINAL REMARKS

GETTING TO WORK WITH THE RIGHT KNOWLEDGE AND TOOLS

In the Netherlands, the 'happiness at work expert' or Chief Happiness Officer is considered a 'profession of the future'. That's great news, seeing as it increases recognition of these experts and highlights the importance of the topic, but by linking it to a specific job title we run the risk of the subject becoming the primary responsibility of a staff department. In fact, happiness is a topic that's relevant for everyone with a job. Everybody is responsible for his or her own happiness at work and everyone should influence the happiness at work of their colleagues. For that reason, we would love to see this profession of Happiness at Work expert, or Chief Happiness Officer, become a role rather than as a profession. A role that anyone can take up, next to his or her 'formal' job title. For that, you need the correct knowledge, skills, and tools.

HAPPY OFFICE MANIFESTO

We have written the Happy Office manifesto, four pillars of a positive work culture to offer a foundation for happiness at work experts and organizations that want to kick off the process of improving happiness at work and building a positive work culture. The book has been constructed in a way that allows you to find the necessary information and practical tips at every desired level (personal, team, or organizational). This book offers you the knowledge, skills and tools required to fulfill the role of CHO. Of course, training and networking with like-minded people is always helpful. The international network of CHO's Woohoo Unlimited is a great source of inspiration and knowledge (www.woohoounlimited.com).

AMBASSADORS OF DIY

In the introduction we already mentioned that we believe change must come from within, that as an organization you must do it yourself. That's why we often refer to ourselves as 'ambassadors of DIY' because we stimulate people in organizations to first get to work themselves and to gather the necessary knowledge and tools. However, that doesn't mean that you don't need external knowledge, help, and guidance throughout the entire change process as you build towards a positive work culture. During the process you will undoubtedly run into specific questions and problems that require an external view or specialist experience. These are the moment when a collaboration between 'internal' and 'external' turns out to be very valuable. And, no, not in the 'old fashioned' way of the external advisor or consultant who comes to tell you how it should be done, but by getting together and supporting where necessary with theoretical backgrounds, research, examples, coaching, tips, and tools. In this way, you can receive support while still ensuring you're directing and controlling your own learning. With that in mind, our change processes always start with training people to become happiness at work experts or positive culture agents. Again, the network of Woohoo Unlimited can help you, with training, talks, workshops and consultants, no matter where you are in the world.

NEED HELP? A TALK, FEEDBACK ON YOUR PLANS, OR INFORMATION ON BECOMING A WOOHOO PARTNER?

Let us know! We are here to help you. After all, it is our purpose to make the world a better place by helping people and organisations spread happiness at work, and to make happiness at work the rule, instead of the exception.

TWELVE OF OUR FAVORITE IDEAS

In this book we have explored many examples of the application of the pillars. Do you need more inspiration? On our website we regularly post ideas that contribute to more happiness at work and a positive work culture (www.happyoffice.nl). This attachment provides you with another twelve of our favorite ideas.

Design the job of your dreams

For: individual
Pillar: purpose (although all pillars play a part in individual happiness)
What does the job of your dreams look like? Few people take the time to think about this while this actually contributes to finding the work that really suits them.

DIY
Think about what you do in the job of your dreams. How do you feel? Which values are important? With whom do you work together? For whom do you do what you do? Make it as specific as possible. Write it down or construct it from Lego. To what extent does this line up with what you are doing now and what can you do to change that?

Anniversary book

For: team/organization
Pillar: purpose

Looking back at the history of the organization helps create connections. During anniversary celebrations and birthdays of the organization it is usually the CEO who explores these stories in speeches. Why not document those stories yourself? We had a client for whom we compiled a book with pictures, stories of their employees, a timeline with the highs and lows of the organization, a timeline with world events, some pictures, and fun facts for each of the ten years the business had existed (which was the anniversary they were celebrating at the time). It became a coffee table book for at home and in the reception area, something to be proud of.

DIY

Make a list of the highs and lows of your team or organization. Ask for input from as many colleagues as possible. Search for stories and pictures of the different moments and see how you shape this moment in time in a beautiful and appropriate way.

Purpose wall

For: team/organization
Pillar: purpose

A cool office does not necessarily contribute to more happiness at work, but it can be helpful when we make visible in our workplace what our work means to us. It feels great when you can realize your personal purpose at your work. For instance, at Rever Interior in the Netherlands, sustainability is of the utmost importance, both in their own office and in the projects they do for their clients. They've set aside one wall in their workplace to make visible what drives employees to excellence. Every employee was asked to choose an object that represented sustainability and the importance thereof for them. The wall has shelves, and they are loaded with all kinds of objects, from bars of Tony's Chocolonely chocolate to Doppers, and sustainable items ranging from carpet to bags. All objects have a sign with the name, a picture, and an explanation of the person for whom this is important and how it reflects in their work.

DIY
Formulate what you as a team think is important, for instance your purpose, and make that visible in a way that speaks to you. Then translate this into a visual: a comic strip, a picture book, a poster, a Game of the Goose, something that you can hang on the wall or make visible one way or the other. Something visible appeals more to emotions than just words.

Bad days are okay!
For: individual
Pillar: people
Happiness at work is not just about being positive and happy all day long. How do you pay attention to this in your own team and convey the message that it is okay to not be happy all the time? At SEB, a pension organization from Denmark, you can indicate your mood with colored cards. When you are cantankerous or angry, you attach a red card to your computer or your coat, a yellow card when you are okay, and a green card when you're happy. In the meantime, colleagues know how they can best help someone when he or she is on 'red'. Do you want to be left alone or does it help when someone gets you a cup of coffee and is willing to lend you an ear?

DIY
For many organizations this type of cards is a bit over the top. But such a mood indicator can contribute to connection at the office. In the Netherlands we see many organizations that do something with a check in at the beginning of the day or a meeting. It often is just about expressing how you feel without having to explain it. You can also make a (physical) mood board with smileys and sad faces.

Employee of the month
For: team/organization
Pillar: people
Another ritual that contributes to a positive work culture is naming an 'Employee of the Month'. With this ritual, employees nominate other colleagues and explain why they think that this person deserves the title. It stimulates people to think about what their colleagues have done in the previous period and what has contributed to everybody's happiness at work. All these motivations/compliments are gathered together and

sent to the colleague concerned. Ultimately a winner is chosen every month, who then receives a prize. It's important to note that winning isn't the point of this exercise! It's more rewarding to receive the compliments—that is what truly contributes to everyone's happiness at work.

DIY
What can you do together to structurally express appreciation and give each other more compliments? Come up together with which custom or ritual is best suitable for that.

Personality Poker
For: team/organization
Pillar: people
Getting to know each other well is important for happiness at work. Playing Personality Poker is a light-hearted and playful way to get to know more about each other's personality and about what makes your colleagues really happy at work. The game offers many leads for good conversations, for instance about the type of feedback that is considered valuable.

DIY
For more information about a session Personality Poker go to our website or https://stephenshapiro.com/personality-poker/

Gratefulness: three good things
For: individual
Pillar: progress
The exercise that is considered by scientists to be the 'most powerful exercise for increased happiness' is all about gratitude. When you are better able to look at the good things in life, your happiness increases considerably. It also decreases your chance of becoming depressed and you are less susceptible to hedonistic adaptation (getting used to good things). You can also apply this exercise to more happiness at work.

DIY
Every day before you go home, write down three things you are grateful for that day. You can do this every day but doing it every week works too. It doesn't matter what you write down! It could be: the sun is shining, a good conversation, an important result, something you recently finished, etc. At first this can

be difficult, but for most people it becomes easier and they get better at it. It would be nice if you would have a buddy for this, like a colleague, so that you can share in each other's gratitude.

Learning from mistakes
For: team/organization
Pillar: progress
We learn most from our own mistakes. You can also learn from each other's mistakes but they must be visible and experienced as positive. That's why it is important to create a culture in which it is safe to make a mistake. At Nixon McInnes they organize the so-called Church of Fail events, where people have to tell everybody what they have done wrong, how they dealt with it, and what they have learned from it. They then receive a standing ovation from the entire audience.

DIY
Come up with a way to discuss the making of mistakes, like making it part of the daily stand-up, team meetings, or by telling stories about it on the internal media.

Open Space Technology
For: team/organization
Pillar: progress
Organize an Open Space Technology conference (OST): do you have a problem for which you would like to have a solution quickly, with input of many employees? During an OST meeting the participants decide the subjects themselves and they come up with solutions together. These sessions can be deployed for small to very large groups and always yield much energy, inspiration, and many good ideas.

DIY
There are a small number of set rules and regulations for an OST meeting. It is important to know those in order to facilitate such a meeting. Do you need help to facilitate an OST conference? By all means, contact us, we love to help.

TRIZ - the Theory of Inventive Problem Solving
For: individual
Pillar: positivity
You can also gain insight into how you can increase your own happiness at work and that of your team by looking at it from a different perspective. One way of doing it is by asking an inverted question and answering it: What are counterproductive activities and behaviours for happiness, and how can we stop them?

DIY
Ask yourself the question: what can I do to make my colleagues unhappy? Make that list as long as possible. After you have finished the list, go through it again and then ask yourself at every point if you have already done this in real life or if you have witnessed it. How can you change that? When you do this exercise as a team, ask yourselves: what can you do as a team to make your colleagues unhappy? Then discuss together what you can do to change things. More of these exercises can be found at www.liberatingstructures.com

Start moving
For: team/organization
Pillar: positivity
Moving is healthy and it positively affects your emotions. Walking a block or two during lunchtime is also good for productivity. One of our clients made maps with different routes to walk in the neighborhood nearby the office, in order to promote walking. The duration and the route are indicated on different maps. These laminated maps are available for everybody at the reception area.

However, there are other options you can explore. For instance, at Experius they hold their one-on-one coaching conversations while walking. More and more companies have standup meetings now, which has the secondary effect of expediting the meetings.

DIY
Would you like to move more with your colleagues? There are several moving challenges that you can participate in. Steptember is one such event, where you are challenged to take

10,000 steps every day during the month of September. You can also keep it small, for instance by doing yoga behind your desk. You can motivate others by posting an article on the intranet or by designing a flyer with a nice story and a number of exercises. You can also organize a yoga session every week. If you really want to be challenged along with your team, then do planks during the next meeting.

Ocean of balloons
For: team/organization
Pillar: positivity
Something to celebrate? At Vega IT in Serbia, they celebrate everything that can be celebrated, and to the fullest. One time, when they achieved a huge success, they filled the entire office with inflated balloons. When they came in, the employees were up to their ankles in balloons and balloons were kicked and thrown around all day. #lol

DIY
What could you do to surprise a colleague or to celebrate the next milepost? Come up with small and larger things on a regular basis to make your colleagues smile. It's often only a small amount of effort but it nets your team a big fun payoff.

www.ingramcontent.com/pod-product-compliance
Lightning Source LLC
Chambersburg PA
CBHW071115160426
43196CB00013B/2573